COOKING TO CONCEIVE THE INCONCEIVABLE

ONE CHEF'S JOURNEY TO FERTILE **FATHERHOOD**

EDWARD N. BAUM

The ideas and tools offered are not meant to replace the advice of an appropriate health professional; they are shared with the understanding that each reader accepts full responsibility for her/his well being.

Adell Press New York

Library of Congress Control Number: 2017903747
ISBN: 978-0-9660078-3-1

Cover design by Susanna Ronner

Photographs by Edward Baum

Manufactured in the United States of America

10 9 8 7 6 5 4 3 2 1

Library of Congress Cataloging-in-Publication Data
Baum, Edward, Cooking to Conceive – 1st ed.
1. Infertility – Male – Popular works.2.Infertility, Male Health –Psychological aspects. 3.Conception – Nutritional Aspects. 4.Fertility, Human – Psychological aspects.

367830118

in memory of
my father

BERNARD BAUM

Contents

3 Forward - Marc Goldstein MD FACS

7 Getting in Line for Seconds

13 A Detour

27 Poised for Warfare

37 The Dancer

51 The Chase is On

57 Snake Oil and Olive Oil

71 The Monster is Coming

83 First Couscous then Paris

93 Such a Brave Boy

103 Da Boys

123 Stand In

131 Sugar and Champagne

143 Production

155 Another Call

161 Sisters

171 Keep Walking Dad; Afterward by Julia Indichova

181 Stories of Hope

197 Some Thoughts on Cooking

207 Recipe Index

209 Fertile Heart Resources

212 Acknowledgments

COOKING TO CONCEIVE THE INCONCEIVABLE

ONE CHEF'S JOURNEY TO FERTILE **FATHERHOOD**

EDWARD N. BAUM

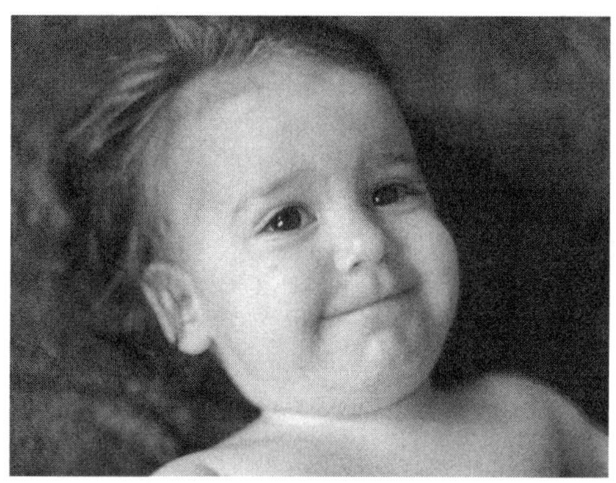

Recipe for a Baby

Getting pregnant is a bit like cooking. The recipe is simple:

1 Egg
200 million Sperm
1 tsp Cervical fluid
1 tsp Seminal fluid

Heat uterus to 98.6°. Combine ingredients. Simmer for nine months. Serves two.

There's one difference between conception and cooking. As essential as temperature and timing might be for a perfect French toast, a burnt or under-cooked breakfast is still food. With a baby, if the flame is too low or your timing is off, you get nothing.

FORWARD

Marc Goldstein, MD, DSc (Hon), FACS
Matthew P. Hardy Distinguished Professor of
Reproductive Medicine and Urology
Surgeon-in-Chief, Male Reproductive Medicine and Surgery
Author of The Couples Guide to Fertility.

Most clinicians would agree that as important as it is to provide our patients with health-related facts, information alone is hardly sufficient to motivate people to make the changes they need to make when they are confronted with a health crisis. If presenting studies was all it would take, no one would smoke, or overeat or resort to drug use. When it comes to galvanizing people to let go of life-long habitual behavior nothing is more effective than a true story of someone who faced similar medical challenges and was healed. Especially when that story is told with as much insight, humor and heart as Edward's wonderful narrative.

What impressed me about Julia and Ed's story in *Cooking to Conceive* as well as when I first read Julia's account of their journey in *Inconceivable*, is how they navigated the rough waters of their diagnoses, and not only conceived an inconceivable baby but profoundly transformed their relationship.

There are many reasons a couple might have difficulty getting or staying pregnant. Although we know that in 40% of cases, infertility is traced to the male partner, for the most part we tend to think of it as a woman's problem. Sadly, I have seen this attitude adversely affect the approach to treatment. The examination in the male is much easier and much less invasive than the examination of the female. Logic would dictate to start the couple's work up with a semen specimen. If that reveals a problem, then we can pursue further investigation.

Unfortunately, I continue to see cases in which the woman has gone through multiple invasive procedures while the husband has only gone through perfunctory testing. Most troubling is to meet couples who discover that not only does the male partner have sperm related issues, he is facing a serious illness which had remained undiagnosed.

As a surgeon, an academic and a researcher, what interests me is how do I employ the sophisticated tests available to me to identify the culprit and then suggest the least invasive approach to addressing the findings of those tests. In our group at Weill Cornell Medicine's Center for Male Reproductive Medicine and Microsurgery we use an assay which in addition to traditional semen analysis determines the percentage of sperm with nicked or damaged DNA. A sperm that has a high percentage of breaks may fertilize the egg but the pregnancy will end in a miscarriage.

During regular IVF, the sperm is deposited near the waiting egg. With damaged sperm, that isn't enough to achieve fertilization. With ICSI, intracytoplasmic sperm injection, we can actually take a problematic or immature sperm and inject it directly into the egg. ICSI is now a widely-used procedure that can circumvent poor sperm quality. Many couples are also using it in the hope that it might improve their chances of a successful pregnancy, but it's a choice that doesn't always serve the best interests of the patient or the child. In recent years, a growing number of studies have shown that babies conceived through ICSI may be at a higher risk for certain birth defects.

So rather than proceed with IVF, or bypass the problem by using ICSI, as a clinician I want to do all I can to first get at the root cause of the fragmentation. It could be an infection, drug or alcohol abuse, varicoceles, one-sided blockages, chronic unremitting stress or a number of intangibles that may affect the quality of the genetic material. Many of these symptoms are treatable. Once treated, the couple can go on to conceive either naturally or with less invasive assistance, like intrauterine insemination.

What is also true, is that a number of these symptoms call for an active participation of the patient. Edward's memoir is a perfect illustration of what I have observed through the years of my own practice. The most important collaborator of the physician is the patient. Listening to our patients, supporting them in becoming more actively engaged in their healing can make a measurable difference in treatment outcome.

Far few narratives speak about the particular physical and emotional challenges of the Dad-to-Be. This is a book every woman caught in the maze of treatments could give to her husband as a compassionate mirror of his own struggles. Emotions which he may not be readily able to articulate.

Inconceivable, Julia and Ed's story told from the vantage point of the female partner, continues to empower thousands of people toward becoming more proactive as they search for solutions, striving to tilt the scale toward a full-term pregnancy. C*ooking to Conceive the Inconceivable* is a much-needed companion book for couples of all genders inspiring them to face a diagnosis as partners intent on being there for each other and strengthening the bonds of their relationship. I look forward to recommending it as a great resource not only for couples facing infertility but any health challenge.

- Marc Goldstein MD, DSc (hon), FACS *New York March 2017*

Chapter One

GETTING IN LINE FOR SECONDS

"What makes the engine go?
Desire, desire, desire."

STANLEY KUNITZ
TOUCH ME

"We need to eat more alkalizing foods," Julia announced brandishing her brand-new copy of "*Alkalize or Die*."

It had been ten months since we were told that we would not be able to have a second child. Ten months of obsessing about our options, ten months of imagining and reimagining life with only one.

"Only one!" The words stung with reproach. In this age of overpopulation, what right did I have to burden the earth with one more set of footprints? Besides, how could I even begin to complain, to be getting in line for seconds with all the hungry, childless couples out there? Can't you see how lucky you are? You already are a dad, I kept telling myself. But I wouldn't listen. Knowing how lucky I was didn't stop me from wanting more.

At first I wasn't taking the diagnoses all that seriously. How could things have deteriorated in such a short time? Ellena, our baby girl, was only ten months old, and we conceived her on the second try.

It was only after I started losing count of doctors and healers that my cavalier mantra of "We can beat this!" morphed into "Can we beat this?" Gradually I stopped accompanying Julia to new appointments. She preferred it that way, wanting to spare me, and I was fine with staying on the sidelines.

But there was one thing I could do. I could cook.

In her quest to overturn the verdict of the experts, my wife appeared to be unstoppable. Coming up with dietary and lifestyle changes aimed at reviving her ovaries had turned our lives into one continuous research project. Julia was the subject and the principal investigator.

I became the chief cook and bottle washer with stellar qualifications for translating her theories into fertility inducing meals.

Before I met Julia, before I gave a thought to marriage and family, I was a professional chef, a proud graduate of the Culinary Institute of America in Hyde Park, New York. It had been several years since I worked in restaurants, but I still loved to cook and spent at least part of most weekends in the kitchen.

So, when Julia came home with her latest list of super-foods, I used them to make dinner, such as an alkalizer-rich squash and beet soup.

Roasted Squash Beet Soup

After cooking this soup I like to pull out the blender. The sensuously smooth puree reminds me of the Haute Cuisine of my past. In keeping with her communist-peasant upbringing Julia likes her soup chunky. Usually I compromise and blend only half the batch.

There are many types of squash and they vary in flavor, not only among varieties but between individual pieces as well. For this recipe, the beets and sweet potatoes should balance out any fluctuation in squash sweetness. Butternut squash is generally sweeter and is a good alternative.

Remember to be cautious if you choose to blend the soup. Do NOT close the lid tight. It's best to keep the small hole in the lid covered only with a clean towel. Hot exploding soup can send you to the hospital with 2nd degree burns, not to mention all the cleanup, if you're still standing.

The kitchen is a dangerous place, sharp knives, hot pots, and hot tempers. Be careful.

3 med **Onions** - ¼" dice (4 cups)
2 tsps **Garlic** - minced
1 tsp **Olive Oil**
1 tsp **Salt**
½ tsp **Pepper**
2 small roasted **Acorn Squash** (2-3 cups)
2 med **Beets** - ¼" dice (2 cups)
1 med-large **Sweet Potato** - ¼" dice (2 cups)
8 cups **Water**

Cut Acorn Squash in half and use a spoon to scoop out the seeds.

Roast at 400 degrees on a slightly Oiled baking tray until soft, 20-30 minutes.

In a large pot sweat Onions (see page 201.)

Add 1 teaspoon Garlic when Onions are translucent.

Add Water and Beets and bring to a boil, then simmer for 30 minutes.

Scoop out roasted Squash from skin using a spoon and add to soup.

Add Sweet Potatoes, return to boil, and then simmer for another 30 minutes.

Finish with Salt, Pepper and remaining Garlic.

Makes 3 quarts.

Chapter Two

A DETOUR

"Every calamity is a spur and a valuable hint."

RALPH WALDO EMERSON
CONDUCT OF LIFE

The three of us lived in a one-bedroom apartment on the Upper West Side of Manhattan. It was a vintage doorman-attended building on Riverside Drive and 100th Street, right across from Riverside Park. We got the place through a friend of a friend who hooked us up with a real estate agent who graciously accepted $1500 cash in an envelope on behalf of the son-in-law of the brother of the landlord. We moved in two months before Ellena was born, and although her crib was in the living room, it was quite spacious compared to our former home in Julia's one-room studio on West 80th Street.

Around Ellena's first birthday we decided to get to work on making her a sibling. Twenty-one months apart seemed like ideal sibling spacing.

It was a Wednesday evening in April, one of Julia's late nights teaching English as a Second Language (ESL) in Queens. I made sure to get home early enough to take over from Vivi, the baby sitter.

I looked forward to those nights home alone with Ellena. At 14 months, she was already a great playmate, and although she preferred constant entertainment, she could occasionally be enticed to sit in a chair for as long as a half hour. The best incentive for achieving this level of cooperation was to offer her something to eat or to play with. A plate of cooked beets, boiled whole until soft then cooled, peeled and sliced, provided both an edible and a toy, leaving me with two available hands for tonight's project: lentil soup.

With Ellena ensconced in her high-chair in the corner of the kitchen, we could keep an eye on each other. Although she was immersed in her beets, she was also keen to keep me in sight as I peeled and chopped.

"The secret is plenty of onions," I told her. "When you think there's too much, add some more." Her face and hands were bright red, and she seemed to fully understand the importance of my proclamation as I waved my knife in the air for emphasis.

With my official onion-chopping goggles on, the exhaust fan humming and Ellena's high chair a safe distance away, I was set to begin. She was unperturbed as I peeled and diced three large onions and scraped them into the pot. Onions are usually cooked with a liberal amount of oil or butter or both. I had come to find this unnecessary. Just enough oil to coat them is sufficient to avoid an acrid smell and flavor. A dash of salt will hasten the process and it won't take long for the onions to start releasing their moisture, otherwise known as sweating, eventually turning translucent.

"You are really going to like this," I exclaimed, sprinkling a little rosemary into the pot. Ellena's gaze followed my fingers.

"You know the Golden Rule, right? Right?" I asked more loudly running towards her chair with the jar of dried rosemary leaves in my hand. "The Golden Rule, right?" Ellena looked up with a knowing smile.

"You can add more, but you can't take away; you can add more, but you can't take away; you can add more, but you can't take away," I chanted louder and louder, whirling around her chair, the jar aloft in one hand. As she tightly clutched a piece of beet in each of her small red hands her eyes chased me around the room.

Then I looked over at the pot on the stove. "They're burning! They're burning!" I yelled, springing toward the sink, and quickly adding a half a cup of water to the pot. This sent up a column of steam, a loud hiss and a fit of giggles from Ellena.

The onions weren't actually burning, just browning slightly. Although this wasn't my original intention, giving the onions some color would bring out a sweet richness that would nicely augment the flavor of the soup. Cooking is, quite often, the skilled revision of an original plan.

Sorting the lentils called for a bit more concentration, but I made sure to check back and forth between Ellena and the stove. The onions needed another stir, and Ellena was still smiling as she clung tightly to her beets, taking pride in the trickle of red liquid running down her wrists.

I was checking for tiny rocks and other debris posing as lentils before rinsing and re-rinsing. After the third rinse I added them to the pot, stirring them into the onions before adding water at about a 4:1 ratio of water to lentils. I turned the burner on high, covered the pot and returned to the counter where four medium carrots awaited me. After a light peeling, I cut them into a small dice, roughly one quarter inch cubes, and then added them to the soup.

Carrot skins can be bitter, and although I feel guilty, I peel them. My guilt stems from a long-held belief that the most nutritious part of a vegetable is the skin. Ever since I began cooking in college I would hear how all the vitamins in a vegetable are in or just below the skin. It turns out this is not exactly true or false. It depends on the vegetable. A cucumber has a skin that is very different in color and texture from the flesh. A different appearance means a different nutritional content. Not necessarily better, but different. Peeling a cucumber will deprive the consumer of all those additional nutrients. Potatoes and eggplants are other good examples. A carrot, however, has a skin that looks very much like the flesh. This indicates that the nutritional content of the skin is not that different from the flesh. A light peeling will not be depriving my family of many nutrients. I guess I'll have to find something else to feel guilty about.

It wasn't long before Ellena sent the plate with the remaining few beets to the floor and held her hands up in my direction with an "I'm done here, Daddy" look in her eyes. I pulled her up from the chair, went back to the stove to lower the now boiling soup to a simmer, then headed for the bathroom to clean us both up before bed. The soup would need another ninety minutes or so cooking at a low simmer.

After a quick wash and change into her favorite giraffe pajamas we headed back to the kitchen. Her head was resting on my shoulder as I warmed up the bottle of breast milk Julia left in the fridge last night. "Nyum" she said.

"That's right," I said. "It's time for milk." Despite being exposed to the word milk in English, Hungarian, Slovak, Russian and Spanish, 'Nyum' was her own creation.

On the way to the rocker I grabbed the first book I spotted. We sat together, reading Zin Zin Violin, a story about an orchestra giving a concert. She fell asleep somewhere between the trombones and the tubas as I continued to rock for a few minutes before carrying her to the crib.

Being with my daughter, especially at bedtime, was a sweet way of slowing down after a day of navigating the complexities of mortgage-backed securities. Although my mind was still reviewing my to-do list, her quiet breathing brought an unexpected wave of gratitude.

I went to the kitchen to check on the soup's progress, giving it a few gentle stirs. If it had begun to burn I wouldn't want to inadvertently dislodge anything sticking to the bottom of the pot. Fortunately, the wooden spoon slid easily across the stainless steel, but the soup was a bit thick, so I added a cup of water and gave it a few more stirs. It wasn't quite done. I could let it simmer for a while. Meanwhile, I turned my attention to the Bear Stearns supplied computer terminal located on a small counter in the kitchen. I turned it on and dialed in to do my nightly checks.

After a few minutes, I heard the front door open. Julia was home early from ESL class. I followed her past our sleeping daughter into the bedroom. She dropped her bag on the bed and turned toward me. She looked scared. Something was wrong.

I could feel my pulse quicken as I braced for impact. "What happened?" I asked.

"I talked to the doctor today," she replied, her eyes welling up with tears. "They said my test results from last week were not actually normal. My hormone levels are too high; the doctor said we'll have trouble having another baby."

We were both still standing as I gently put my arms around her and held her until the tears she must've fought all day subsided.

My mind was racing. How could this be? It's only been a year since Ellena was born, conceived on the second try. Should I really be concerned? It was just one test. Was it definitive? Should we take it seriously?

"If only we had started right after Ellena's birth," Julia asserted. "They say that's the most fertile time. We should've known!"

I could easily have joined her in self-flagellation. We were both pretty good at that, but that wasn't what she needed right then. On the bright side, I was able to defer facing my own feelings in the interest of consoling her.

"We couldn't have moved any faster," I softly said. "We weren't ready. Everything will work out. Do you remember when we first held Ellena, how tiny she was? How easy it was to love her? We'll love this baby no matter where it comes from."

"He said we should see a specialist," Julia explained, another wave of tears threatening to descend. "There's got to be something they can do, don't you think?"

"Of course," I said, "Why else would he tell you to see a specialist? We will do whatever it takes. If we really want another child, we'll find a way."

We held each other for several minutes in silence. Meanwhile my mind was rocketing between fear and disbelief. The image of my future family, the image I'd taken for granted ever since I envisioned having a family, was suddenly yanked away by some random blood test. I had always thought there would be four of us: two parents, two children. A playmate for Ellena. A sibling. I didn't want my daughter to be an only child.

It was a given. It had always just been a question of how many years would they be apart.

"It's just one test," I said. "We just did this a year ago; we'll do it again."

Did I believe it, or was I mouthing these words not just to comfort my wife but to mask my own fear? The voice of reassurance is one I am familiar with. I use it a lot.

After a while, Julia seemed to be unclenching. It was hard to tell. Maybe it was just me tensing up.

She opened the door to peek in on Ellena, and the smell of the cooking lentils jolted me back to the soup. I ran to the kitchen.

It was a little thick, but the lentils weren't burnt—not even sticking to the pot. Julia had followed right behind and smiled watching me stir the soup. "Is that lentil soup?" She asked pulling off her sweater. "I am really hungry. Is it ready to eat?"

"Almost," I replied. I stirred, tasted, added some salt, tasted, added some black pepper and chopped garlic, stirred some more, tasted and then finished up with the magic ingredient: soy sauce.

After one last approving taste, I ladled some out into a bowl on top of some leftover brown rice and handed it to her.

"I'll eat this in the bath," Julia said, burying her face in my neck. Then she turned and, soup in hand, headed off to the bathroom.

I spent the next 30 minutes cleaning up the kitchen and dividing the soup into containers, half of which were destined for the freezer. (Later, when defrosting them, I would add a bit more garlic and soy sauce to each.) My work with the soup was distracting me from Julia's news, which was a blessing. I didn't usually do such a thorough job cleaning up.

I had to pass Ellena's crib on the way to our bedroom. I lingered for a moment watching her. She was on her back with one arm folded over her chest, her head touching the belly of her favorite stuffed panda, Bee-0. Ellena's steady breathing was calming. I walked to the bedroom and closed the door quietly. I could hear the water still running and opened the bathroom door to find Julia lying in a half-full bath with her leg dangling over the side of the tub.

"Unbelievable soup!" she smiled. "I will call Lisa tomorrow. They've been trying to have a kid for years. She's got to know the best in the business. Money is no object for them."

I reached for my toothbrush. "I'm sure you're not the only one. This has to be a common problem; they must know how to deal with it," I said. Exhaustion collided head on with the night's news. I felt utterly drained and struggled to keep my eyes open.

"Please go to bed. I'm really fine; I'll call Lisa in the morning," said Julia, motioning me to come towards to her.

She did seem calmer. I leaned over the bath and pressed my face against her hair. She put her hand in mine, and we stayed still for several moments. I kissed her head and went off to bed.

I lay under the covers, exhausted but unable to sleep. In my mind I listed all the couples I knew with only one child. Were they happy? Would I be OK staying in that club? I thought about a colleague and his wife who were smitten with their newly adopted baby girl from Peru. I thought about my friends Leonard and Ruthie who loudly defended their non-breeder status. But were they being honest? Both of them?

Julia eventually slipped carefully into bed trying not to wake me. I wrapped myself around her and whispered, "We will get through this."

"I was mostly nervous about telling you," she admitted "I want another child—for me yes, and a sister for Ellena of course, but mostly I want one for you."

Was that true? Did I want another child more than Julia did? Was this really more important to me? Was it all about my image of a perfect family of two adults and two kids? If you had asked me before if I wanted another child, I would have certainly said yes. But why? Why did it now feel like such an acute yearning? I didn't have much more than a superficial answer for that question.

A cry from the living room interrupted my thoughts. A sweet cry. Ellena was stirring, and Julia swiftly rose to comfort her. It felt as though that cry was helping me find answers to my questions. As long as we could remind each other how blessed we were with our one healthy, blue-eyed baby girl, we'd get through this with a lot less angst. Or so I hoped as I finally drifted off to sleep.

A distant voice, what were they saying? Were they talking to me? It took a few moments to get my bearings. It was my clock radio telling me it was 6:15. It seemed earlier. As I went through the familiar motions of my morning routine, an ache in my gut brought back the news of the previous night.

Julia and Ellena were still sleeping as I tiptoed out of the apartment. My morning commute from the Upper West Side to Midtown was two short subway rides sandwiched between two five minute walks. Leaving by 7:00 meant a less crowded and faster number 3 train. Thankfully, the cafeteria was practically empty at that hour. I got to toast and butter my sesame bagel, pour out an extra-large cup of hazelnut coffee and walk to my desk without gazing into a familiar face.

My cubicle was comfortable, and the early morning quiet made it easier to breathe. "Pay attention to your breath," I told myself. I counted three in-breaths then looked around. Thankfully I was still alone. What was I working on? After reading a few emails and listening to several phone messages, I was soon pulled back to the world of Fixed Income Databases.

I am a computer programmer for the Financial Analytics and Structured Transactions Group at Bear Stearns. I work with data and databases, mostly mortgages. We keep tabs on millions of loans for homes and cars and businesses. These loans are sold from savings banks to investment banks like Bear Stearns, packaged in various ways and then resold to investors. It's all very complicated and couldn't be done without computers or computer programmers. Although I work long hours, I do mostly get weekends off.

Becoming a programmer was basically Julia's idea. When we met I was working as a chef in a midtown restaurant. Julia didn't have much confidence in my ability to support a family and told me so with characteristic frankness. That conversation led to me feeling deeply insulted and thinking our two-month-old relationship was over. Which led to me going back to my apartment alone and contemplating being single again.

Which led to Julia knocking on my door several hours later, confessing that in a moment of self-destructive anxiety she'd said the wrong thing. Which led to a lot of crying and passionate love-making. Which led to me talking to my best friend Jeff, a computer programmer, about learning programming. Which led to a certificate program at Columbia University. Which led to reverse commuting to eastern Long Island for a year at my first programming job. Which led to Jeff arranging an interview at his firm. Which led to me getting a better-paid, closer job in midtown Manhattan, down the hall from him, managing a database with the information on 40 million home loans.

I have often been asked if I miss the restaurant business. "Not really," I reply. "I get to cook for an appreciative clientele on a regular basis."

I truly enjoy cooking: the creation and execution, the sharing and consumption. I also enjoy programming: the problem solving, the creation and execution. On the surface they are quite different, yet there are many similarities. Cooking and programming are both stimulating and immersive. As I would tell prospective employees at Bear Stearns, "When I look at my watch I don't say 'Oh man, it's only 2 o'clock,' I say 'Oh man, it's already 2 o'clock.'" The restaurant business was the same way. There was never enough time.

At its heart a computer program is a recipe. It's a linear, start-to-finish self-contained unit, with an intended outcome. Unfortunately, like a casserole, at times the result is not what you had in mind. Both computers and meals can generate last-minute crises that demand swift solutions. Mortgage traders need their data, and diners need their lunch. There's no way to tell them to "wait till tomorrow."

My friend Jeff stopped by my cubicle on the way to his office. I wondered if I looked tired, worried, infertile? "Hey, good morning, I just want to let you know that I can't make lunch today. I've got to be downtown," he said.

"OK, maybe tomorrow." Nothing else was said for the moment.

I decided not to discuss Julia's test results. It was tough to keep from thinking about them, but as the day went on I began to lose myself in the puzzles, conundrums and tasks of mortgage trading data. In my cubicle I was a master troubleshooter. I could track down and debug most problems faster than anyone. Work was a moderately effective neutralizer of my helplessness. I was in control there and, at least for the moment, the ache in my gut had lost its edge.

Lentil Soup

There are many types of lentils: brown, red, French (green), regular. Many health food stores, specialty shops and large groceries or supermarkets have a variety. The French or Green variety, are smaller, stay a little firmer and maintain their shape longer. I recommend trying out the different types to see which ones you prefer. The cooking method is the same, but the time needed to cook them will vary slightly.

3 med **Onions** - ¼" dice (4 cups)
2-3 med-large **Carrots** - ¼" dice (2 cups)
1 small **Sweet Potato** - ⅛" dice (1 cup)
1 Tbsp **Garlic** minced
1 Tbsp **Olive Oil**
1 tsp **Sweet Paprika**
1 tsp **Rosemary** Leaves (fresh if possible)
1 tsp **Salt**
½ tsp **Black Pepper**
2 tsps **Soy Sauce/Tamari** (optional)
1 pound **Lentils (2 ½ cups)**
8 cups **Water**

In a large pot sweat Onions (see page 201.)

Add half the Garlic when Onions become translucent.

Wash the Lentils and add to the Onions and Garlic, stir well and then add the Water.

Add Carrots, Sweet Potatoes, Salt, Paprika and Rosemary.

Bring to a boil, then lower heat and simmer approximately 90 minutes.

Using a wire whisk will do a better job of blending the Lentils and Sweet Potatoes, making for a more creamy texture.

Finish with Soy Sauce to taste. I like using salt during the cooking process, seasoning just under the desired saltiness and then finish with Soy Sauce before serving.

Makes 3 quarts.

Chapter Three

POISED FOR WARFARE

"To be nobody but yourself in a world which is doing its best, night and day, to make you everybody else means to fight the hardest battle which any human being can fight; and never stop fighting."

E.E. CUMMINGS
A POETS ADVICE

Julia was poised for warfare. Within a week of endless phone calls and convoluted connections, we were scheduled to meet our first specialist. Doctor C was near the top of Julia's list; his credentials were impeccable, and he was willing to see us. This sounded promising, since the first two physicians refused to meet with us after hearing Julia's numbers. They couldn't help. They said that a consultation would have been a waste of money and time.

In preparation for our first consult, we had to find out if, in addition to Julia's soaring hormone levels, I was in any way contributing to the problem. Doctor C recommended a lab for testing my sperm. Luckily, an appointment was available the next day. The lab was ten minutes from my office. A quick visit would not interfere too much with my work day.

I arrived a few minutes early. Three middle-aged women in white coats sat in a hospital grey, brightly lit office. The blonde in the middle barely looked up from her papers as she waved me to my seat in a small waiting room. I didn't have much time to conjure up stories about the men and women seated around me because a nurse called my name soon after I sat down. I could feel everyone's eyes upon me as I was handed a cup and led down the hall.

"Make sure you get it all in the cup," she said matter-of-factly, "and please hold the cup on the outside only. Skin oils affect the test."

I nodded.

"Just bring it to the desk when you are done."

I was left alone in what appeared to be a typical examination room, except for the stacks of Playboy and Penthouse magazines. My first concern was that Miss February would not have a strong enough appeal amidst the fluorescent lighting and crinkly exam table paper. Another smaller yet not insignificant concern was that I shouldn't do this too quickly. What, I wondered, was the expected length of time for sexual arousal and climax in a laboratory setting? I was convinced that everyone on the other side of the door had clicked the start button on their stop watches, evaluating my performance.

It turned out that my teenage years of practice hadn't been wasted after all, and I was able to meet my production quota within what I deemed to be an appropriate amount of time—not conspicuously long nor a publicly premature ejaculation either. I handed my sealed sample cup to the blonde at the desk and fled.

Ten minutes later I was in my cubicle but unable to focus on my work for the rest of the day. Our first appointment with a specialist, one of the best in the field, was the next day. A barely audible voice in my head kept repeating the same mantra. "We will get this fixed."

The next day I was running a little late and arrived at Doctor C's waiting room just as Julia's name was being called. A young unsmiling assistant led us into the doctor's office, where we were greeted by a man straight out of the cast of General Hospital: fiftyish and fit, with a graying full head of hair—someone I would be proud to call my doctor. The sparsely furnished room itself, with its burnished wooden desk and solemn medical textbooks, seemed to be saying, "You're in good hands here. I'll take over now; you can relax." Phew! The picture on the desk of the attractive woman holding two little girls echoed the same message: "Trust me. I know what I'm doing."

Doctor C appeared unruffled as Julia apprehensively answered his basic questions about her reproductive history. Her first pregnancy, Ellena's birth and her current cycles were all met with approving nods.

"Forty-two is high. Very high," he said looking at the infamous lab report.

There was a pause before Julia asked, "Couldn't the number just drop on its own?"

"Of course it could," the physician answered. "But..."

Hadn't I been adequately prepared for this "but"? Didn't at least part of me suspect that it wouldn't be easy?

"The fact that it even once went up this high is discouraging."

I felt numb as Dr. C. discussed our options. "False hope" and "poor prognosis" were two phrases that drowned out the rest of his comments. I looked at Julia who appeared to not have heard those words. Or did she? She seemed to be patiently awaiting a suggestion of treatment options.

He wanted us to meet with the staff psychologist.

Our first specialist then stood up, signaling an end to our meeting.

"Hope we can help," he said, coming around his mighty desk to shake our hands.

Did he? Did he really hope he could help? I asked myself as we left his office. Why then did I have the distinct feeling that the moment he saw that damned number on Julia's lab report, he'd lost interest in the rest of our story?

Julia and I returned to the packed waiting room and took the two remaining seats in the corner. I must not let Julia sense my disillusionment, I thought, sliding my hand into hers. She looked at me with an uncertain smile. "You really don't have to stay anymore," she said quietly.

I shook my head. "I'm OK."

It didn't take that long for our names to be called again, this time by a well-manicured thirty-something woman in a deep-blue tailored suit who seemed out of place amidst all the white coated medical personnel. She led us to her office which was decorated with colorful diagrams and plastic models of the female reproductive system.

After scanning our chart, a professional, reserved smile crossed her face. "The good news is, you're not in menopause," she said brightly, looking at my expressionless wife.

"Does that mean we can have another baby?" Julia inquired.

I listened intently, hoping someone with some authority would contradict what we'd been hearing.

"Unfortunately, no," was the measured response.

Then there were more words, but I was no longer paying attention. I found myself staring at the plastic models of a uterus and ovaries on her desk. I caught a few more phrases about egg donation, adoption, surrogacy. Then there were the business cards of adoption lawyers and egg donor specialists before she, too, stood up, letting us know that she had done her part.

I wanted to cut through all this euphemism and politeness so the meeting wouldn't be a total waste. "Do you know of anyone who has conceived with Julia's numbers?" I asked.

"No, there are no documented cases," she replied, this time more softly, genuinely pained about delivering this upsetting final verdict.

Julia and I were on the street before I spoke. "When in doubt, have some *palacsintas*," I announced. "Mocca is just three blocks from here."

"But you should get back to work," Julia objected.

"It's OK, I told them I would be a while."

We headed uptown. I felt deflated, as if someone had slashed my tires. My expectations had been up—maybe not through the roof, but up.

Julia hooked her arm under my elbow and said, "I have other names, other doctors; I will get another appointment."

Was my warrior wife attempting to reassure me, or was she really as unfazed by these dismal encounters as she appeared to be? Whether or not it was a brave front or true equanimity, her attitude had a calming effect.

"I will make some calls," she added confidently.

The Hungarian restaurant, Mocca, is a little bit of the Old Country right here in Manhattan. *Chicken Paprikash*, stuffed peppers, *palacsintas* and Julia's favorite—poppy seed noodles. But Mocca is more than exotic eastern European entrees. It is familiarity and warmth and comfort, especially for Julia, who grew up in Czechoslovakia with Hungarian Jewish parents. Even I feel comforted here, and I'm a Brooklyn boy. We visited Hungary when Julia was pregnant with Ellena—a surreal voyage for both of us. Most of the country seemed frozen in time from the height of the Soviet hegemony, the ultimate in tacky grandeur. Mocca is like being there again, minus the musty carpeting.

I was tempted by the stuffed peppers but ordered the *palacsintas* instead. They are basically crepes with a colorful fruit filling. Julia ordered the poppy seed noodles. We've made them at home. The ingredients are simple: flat noodles, poppy seeds, butter and sugar. Julia likes to add apricot jam.

First thing to consider when attempting poppy seed noodles is to get good seeds. If they are stale or even just slightly old, you might as well not bother. Fortunately, there's a shop right next door to Mocca where we buy fresh poppy seeds by the pound, which I reminded Julia to do before going home.

Mocca makes some great dishes, and their noodles are tasty, but I do like ours better. Actually, the recipe is from Julia's mother. I start with butter in a pan, add the seeds and cook under low heat, stirring frequently. (Make sure not to let the butter brown!) After about 5 minutes add the apricot jam. Then mix in the cooked noodles and cover. We do more or less the same thing with gnocchi, this being a somewhat reasonable stand-in for the Slovak potato dumplings of my wife's youth. The main concern with gnocchi is to avoid overcooking and more importantly, over-handling.

Mocca did the trick. Just sitting in that corner booth waiting for our food, I felt myself thawing out. "You were right; this is exactly what we needed," Julia smiled. She was consoling me, and I was grateful—partly because I could take a break from consoling her. Clearly, she saw this crisis as her problem. I could sense her fierce determination to spare me any pain. She rubbed my shoulders, erasing that disheartening doctor's visit. Then suddenly the words came back in my mind: "There are no documented cases of women getting pregnant with an FSH of 42." I anxiously repeated them to Julia.

"What about all the undocumented cases?" She shot back.

She was poised for warfare, all right, and I had just received my draft notice.

Chia Pudding

Chia seeds are a true super food. They are high in nutrients and low in calories, and a good source of anti-oxidants and omega-3 fatty acids, more per gram than salmon.

3 cups **Coconut Milk** (or other non-dairy milk substitute)
½ cup **Chia Seeds**
2 tsps **Maple Syrup** or **Honey**
½ tsp **Vanilla**
pinch **Salt**
Fruit (Berries, Peaches, Pitted Cherries...)

Combine all ingredients, except Fruit, in a medium-sized bowl and stir until completely mixed.

Cover and refrigerate for at least 4 hours or better yet, overnight.

Add in Fruit when serving.

Serves 6-8.

Chapter Four

THE DANCER

"O body swayed to music, O brightening glance,
How can we know the dancer from the dance?"

WILLIAM BUTLER YEATS
AMONG SCHOOL CHILDREN

Millions of mortgage-backed securities required constant attention and provided a welcome escape from the reality of the Park Avenue infertility specialists. Julia, on the other hand was undistractable. Her sense of purpose and her laser focus were the same traits I recognized the very first time I saw her.

It was a hot and sticky late summer Friday in Manhattan as we boarded the 4:32 Bay Shore Express from Penn Station.

An invitation to spend three days on Fire Island arrived at the same time as a mid-August heat wave. My friend Pam had a half-share in a house in the town of Fair Harbor, and she had not yet exhausted her guest quota.

Pam was interested in being more than friends. I was not. She made it clear that she wouldn't tolerate me hooking up with any of her housemates; the invitation was contingent on my agreeing to play by Pam's rules. I told myself if I ever got near it, I'd figure out a way to cross that bridge. It was a small price to pay for avoiding heat prostration on the sidewalks of New York.

We were part of a crowd streaming off the Long Island Railroad and piling into taxis for the short ride to the Ferry Terminal. Boats destined for various Fire Island towns were waiting to receive their passengers and squire them to idyllic seaside vacations.

We purchased our tickets and boarded the boat. There were plenty of seats outside since the wind-averse regulars were ensconced in their usual spots in the cabin. As we pulled away from Long Island I could feel the temperature dropping and the burdens of the week lifting off my shoulders. Attractive weekenders sat in rows of benches, holding cans of Heineken or books, or both. It occurred to me as I watched the dock fade from view that Pam's housemates wouldn't be the only women on the island.

The thirty-minute-ride seemed much shorter. As we disembarked into a waving and hugging crowd, welcoming friends and lovers, I could see rows and rows of little red wagons, the kind you pulled when you were six. The new arrivals unloaded their luggage, totebags and groceries from the mainland onto the wagons, pulling them along as they walked the few blocks to their houses. The streets of Fire Island are car-free and are actually not streets at all but boardwalks. Children on bicycles meander from the beach back to their houses or to the market without supervision. On Fire Island, it's always 1962.

I was a guest in a houseful of single thirty-somethings who made their semi-monthly pilgrimage to sun, sand, parties and, above all, the hope of romance. Activities on the Island included lying on the beach (but rarely swimming), bar-hopping by way of water-taxi and drinking designer vodka. Sandwiched between afternoon sunbathing and a night of prowling was dinner. Each timeshare had its own dinner dynamics. In Pam's house, everyone ate together and everyone helped prepare the meals.

Fair Harbor's food market might have been the only game in town but they knew their clientele. With an abundance of fresh produce, fish, meats and baked goods, it was a perfect one-stop shopping venue. Like all of the regulars, we had already factored the absurdly high prices into the cost of the vacation. Perusing the bounty on display, our group weaved through the aisles, considering our options. After Pam, with more than a hint of pride, acknowledged my culinary background, everyone happily deferred to me. And I just as happily took charge.

The asparagus looked fresh; the salmon not so much. Freshly butchered chicken thighs would be great for grilling. Sweet corn, Bib lettuce, hothouse cucumbers, peppers and tomatoes rounded out our meal. We were not short on ingredients.

Back at the house a team was standing by, awaiting instructions. Actually, they were sitting around drinking margaritas, but with a slight nudge were ready to start cooking. Donning my invisible *Toque Blanche*—no longer just a guest—I was ready to get to work.

Had it been only three months since Current closed? My first and only foray into restaurant ownership had been a wild ride. I was still decompressing from that all-too-brief stint as partner and chef. It felt like a previous incarnation.

On Monday October 19, 1987, the New York Stock Exchange experienced the largest percentage drop ever in its history. I had spent that day getting ready for dinner service at Current, the Soho New York seafood restaurant of which I was Chef and one-eighth owner. It was our busiest Monday in the year we'd been open, and I remarked how the crash might not be so bad for business. I was wrong.

I met Mike in 1979 while interning as a prep cook halfway through my education at the Culinary Institute. I looked up to him as a chef, teacher and mentor. A few years later he opened Gann, a Nouvelle-French-Japanese Restaurant and spent two years trying to educate the public in fusion cuisine. He was slightly ahead of his time and not quite the best marketer, which is why one day he approached me about becoming one of three new partners in Gann. It wooneuld be a new direction, a new concept, a new design and an influx of much needed cash. I would put up ten thousand dollars and become the Chef de Cuisine. Francoise would add ten thousand more and become the Maître D', and for his ten thousand, Larry the Lawyer would be able to say he was a restaurateur. Mike would maintain majority control and oversee. After three weeks of renovation, the upscale, sedate Gann was turned into a slick, hip seafood joint called Current. A tile mosaic behind the bar and large hanging art pieces by Peter Kitchell were meant to fit in with all the neighborhood art galleries. It was, after all, in the heart of Soho.

Our initial menu featured several different fish and sauce options, the idea being that the customers could mix and match their favorite sauce with their favorite fish. It did not go over well. I was surprised to learn that most people preferred less choice. They were constantly asking which was the best sauce for each fish. We abandoned the idea

three weeks after opening.
Francoise had some trouble coming up with the cash, and he only lasted nine days. Begrudgingly, Mike took over the front-of-the-house, and I nervously kicked in eight thousand dollars more. After a few months, Mike suggested that I leave the kitchen and do a couple of nights a week being the front-man, managing the dining room. I resisted but eventually bought a few new shirts and got out there. Surprisingly, I liked it and soon wound up working the majority of nights on the floor. It was the first time in my restaurant career that I got to spend time with the customers. When friends came in, and it wasn't too busy, I could pull up chair and join them for a drink. It was actually my job, in addition, of course, to managing staff, greeting guests, taking orders, bussing dishes, tending bar, mopping spills and basically doing anything and everything that needed to get done.

After being open a year, we were just beginning to shows signs of success, but the market crash squashed that. We were always just a half-step ahead of the creditors. Occasionally they would catch up, like the day the New York State Tax Authority showed up with a chain and padlock and only left after being handed a $4000 cashier's check. Months passed slowly with random busy nights and occasional signs that business was indeed improving. Then on one nice spring day Mike informed me he was leaving the restaurant.

"What am I supposed to do?" I asked.

He just shrugged.

I was quite depressed the rest of the day. Despite our dire finances, I had been clinging to the hope that we could get through this. On the long taxi ride home, I realized that Mike was right—leaving Current wouldn't be such a bad idea.

The next day he was sitting in the office when I came in. "I thought about it a lot and decided that I am OK with you leaving, in fact I am OK with you doing whatever you would like here, because I'm leaving too."

I walked away. It was a relief but it wasn't easy. I had failed. I blamed Mike for not being honest, for using a good chunk of the money to pay off old debts, leaving us with little cash to get past the renovation. I blamed the economy which hit most New York restaurants pretty hard, and I blamed myself for not persevering. I could have done more, I could have made it work, if only I had… It was painful but also liberating to walk away. I was feeling both ends of the emotional spectrum: elation, depression and pretty much everything in between. I felt numb. I was no longer a restaurant owner, but I was confident I would get another chance.

It was May 7th 1988.

Pam's voice brought me back to the present.

"OK Chef, we're ready."

"Who wants to chop garlic?" I asked. "We need a lot."

"I can do that," Lisa volunteered. "I'm Italian."

"And I can wash the Lettuce," Pam added. "I'm Jewish."

We were all still laughing when I called Andrea over for a knife demo on dicing the tomatoes and cucumbers. Steve also wanted to help, and after another quick demo, he began cautiously slicing the red, green and yellow peppers.

I looked around the room. My five assistants were happily chopping, slicing and peeling as the music of Brian Ferry and Roxy Music wafted in from the living room. I grabbed a Bass Ale from the cooler and took a sip. I thought back to my days at the CIA and the classes where we would taste and analyze various wines and beers. Classes where our palates were taught to discern complex flavors. I could imagine discussing the beer I was holding in my hand, that it had a rich caramel sweetness, followed up with biscuit malt and a fruity bite, but now all I could feel was a wave of joy as the cool

liquid flowed through me.
It doesn't get a whole lot better than this, I thought.

There was plenty of food, but would there be enough? Just to make sure, another dish seemed like a good idea. After noticing a couple of cans of College Inn chicken broth, I remembered a great recipe for stuffing. Who doesn't like, good ol' Thanksgiving Day stuffing? John and Alice were still on the couch with their margaritas, and fortunately not too wasted to bike to the market for a few loaves of bread.

Aside from the bread, stuffing meant more chopping: onions, celery, parsley. I delegated these tasks to Lisa and Pam. Steve was still on the peppers.

It was time to start cooking. "Anybody know how to start the grill?" I asked.

John volunteered. Meanwhile, we'd have to settle for a quick fifteen-minute marinade for the chicken thighs: olive oil, soy sauce, honey, rosemary and red pepper flakes. I decided to grill the fresh corn first with their husks on, which would steam the kernels while adding a bit of smokiness from the charred leaves.

A new volunteer, Jane, showed up just in time for the asparagus. I instructed her on the intricacies of trimming the delicate vegetable. "Cut off about an inch of the bottoms and then peel the lower third. The thicker the stalk the more we need to peel to avoid that woody texture," I said as I demonstrated. "We'll finish by brushing them with olive oil and garlic and throwing them on the grill, but let's wait till the rest is done."

Lisa was now available to sauté the onions, celery and garlic for the stuffing. After they lightly browned, we transferred them to large bowl and let them cool before adding three eggs, a quart of canned chicken stock, a little white wine and the cubed bread. I set the oven to 350 and put in the stuffing.

It took another 45 minutes before the dinner bell was sounded, but less than a minute to gather the twelve of us around the long table. There we were, a bunch of single professionals—eating, chatting, laughing, enjoying this incredible bounty. The chicken was tender, slightly charred and a bit spicy from the red pepper flakes. The corn was sweet with a hint of smoke and perfectly cooked. The fresh basil gave the stuffing a dash of sweetness complimenting the garlic and thyme. In fact, the stuffing was the hit of the meal, giving the chicken a festive accent and harkening back to family holiday tables.

After the food and the wine had settled and the kitchen was pretty well cleaned up, six of us headed over to Joe's Dock. Restaurant by day and dance club at night, Joe's was the place to be in Fair Harbor—its best and only nightclub. The tables and chairs from the night's dinner service were pushed aside, exposing a fair-sized wooden dance floor that quickly filled with bodies. We made our way through the pulsating crowd to a relatively empty corner as Michael Jackson gave way to the Temptations. We had no partners as we danced, weaving in and out of circles, twosomes and threesomes. It felt good to be moving, interacting, flirting, trading dance moves and smiles with my new friends.

I have a special reverence for dancers and an appreciation for dance partners who listen with their bodies and help coax the dancer in me out of hiding. In one of our comprehensive talks about women, my friend Robert and I agreed that good lovers are not necessarily good dance partners, but a good dance partner has a pretty good shot at working out as a lover.

Marvin Gaye followed The Temptations, which led into Earth, Wind and Fire. The bass lines and rhythmic hooks were gathering steam and keeping us all moving. I reminded myself to compliment the DJ. Barry left us to head to the bar, and I attempted to give equal dancing attention to Pam, Maggie, Sue and Jane.

Then I saw her: a woman in white—white tank top, white drawstring pants—with reddish hair. She was dancing with a couple of other women. Not exactly dancing, but living the music. Bass, treble and her. In the darkness, I couldn't see her that clearly, but I could see her move, her arms sweeping through the air. I couldn't look away. I was hooked.

Her focus was absolute. Letting the music move through her, she seemed to have blocked out everything aside from the sound and rhythm of the songs. Still, I had a sense that she must have known I was watching. She must have known how badly I wished to dance towards her and let our bodies harmonize in a call-and-response. She must've known how tough it had been for me to find a partner to play and share and dance with. She must have known that the women I was dancing with were not really my "partners." She must have known that I was simply being a thoughtful guest, and as such, couldn't simply abandon my hosts.

And she must have known that I was watching as she left the club. Through the nearby window I could see her walk down the street and out of my life.

A missed opportunity.

The next day, my housemates and I packed up and headed back to the city. I looked for the Woman-in-White on the dock and the ferry and the train. She was nowhere to be seen. In the days that followed, I couldn't get Fair Harbor, dancing at Joe's and the mysterious woman out of my mind. Yet another item for my list of what-ifs.

Two weeks later, Pam called. "Eddie, are you busy tomorrow? Would you like to come back out to Fair Harbor for a few days?" She asked. "Everyone is still talking about the stuffing!"

Being a professional chef opens many doors. Two days later I was back on the deck of the ferry watching Fire Island come into focus.

Three days of sun and sea and water taxis and collective dinners rushed by, as I kept one eye out for the Woman-in-White. Friday came too quickly, and in keeping with the late afternoon custom in Fair Harbor, I joined a group from the house with drinks in hand and headed over to the ferry dock. It had been a good visit, despite not finding the love of my life. As we walked over, I thought about my original agreement with Pam to avoid any intimacy with her housemates. I wondered if that had really been in my interest.

Hints of red and orange streaked the sky as the crowd sipped cocktails, mingling and searching for connections that may have been missed earlier. I was sitting on a railing slightly to the side, sufficiently aloof to the general scene. I was able to watch the crowd, secure in the knowledge that I really didn't belong. After all, I was just visiting. I was just about to leave the dock to prepare for my departure when I saw her. The Woman-in-White. I was frozen. She stood with a small group, a mug instead of a margarita in her hand. She was wearing white again, maybe even the same pants she wore on the dance floor and a white zippered sweatshirt. My heart was picking up speed; I had been imagining this encounter for two weeks. Now that my prayers had been answered, I was unable to move. For a brief moment, I considered pretending I hadn't noticed—but no, I had to gather the courage to act, otherwise she'd stay on that list of regrets forever. If only she wasn't standing with all those other people. Maybe I could just wait until she separated from her friends. Two minutes seemed like two hours as I considered my options. I was sweating. I had to do this. I decided not to wait for her to break free.

I walked over. She was facing away from me.

"Excuse me," I said, trying to get her attention. She didn't make it easy. Turning slightly toward me, she stepped forward to let me pass.

I held my ground and repeated, "Excuse me." This time she turned to face me.

"Hi," I said, "I just wanted to tell you that you are a wonderful dancer."

She looked puzzled.

"I saw you dancing at Joe's the other night."

"Oh." Her face relaxed into a smile. She was on the smallish side, but well proportioned. She had soft brown eyes that were intently checking me out.

I wasn't sure what name to use, Ed, Eddie, Edward. "My name is Ed," I said.

We discussed our tenure on the Island, how the summer was coming to a close. She sipped from her mug, and the scent of chamomile tea mixed with the salty air and assorted colognes, perfumes and hygiene products from the crowd surrounding us. Her

voice was foreign.
"So, what other language do you speak?" I asked, attempting to impress her with my keen observation.

"I speak a few others," she replied coyly.

"How many?"

"Oh, five or six."

"Well, is it five or six?"

She smiled. "It depends. How old are you?" She asked.

Her question didn't seem odd. "Thirty-two, how about you?"

"Thirty-eight." It didn't raise any flags.

Although it was the start of the Labor Day holiday, I was leaving the island on the last ferry because guests, no matter how well they cooked, were not allowed on holiday weekends. I didn't have much time.

"Maybe we could go dancing in the city sometime?" I asked.

She smiled and nodded in agreement.

We walked back to her house so she could give me her phone number. Ordinarily there was no reason to bring a pen or paper to the dock. I felt like the most recent catch on display as her housemates gave me the once- and twice-over.

The last ferry leaving the island was nearly empty. I was one of only nine sleepy passengers watching the Fair Harbor dock fade from view as we chased the last bit of daylight to the west. In my pocket was the phone number of a foreigner who didn't look Jewish, but could most definitely dance. Her name was Julia.

Kale and Sweet Potato Sauté

This is simple, quick and has a great combination of flavors.

1 large **Sweet Potato** - grated (3 cups)
1 head **Kale**, about 12 -15 large leaves - 1" dice
1 ½ tsp **Coconut Oil**
1 ½ tsp **Olive Oil**
1 tsp **Garlic** - minced
½ tsp **Salt**
pinch **Cayenne Pepper** (to taste)

In a large pan add Garlic and Coconut and Olive Oil.

Cook with med-high heat until Garlic starts to brown.

Quickly add Sweet Potatoes and stir well with wooden spoon.

Mix well, coating the Potatoes with the Oil and Garlic.

Add Kale – stir and cover for 1 minute, stir again and cover until cooked.

Season to taste with Salt and Cayenne and stir very well – be careful, a little Cayenne goes a long way.

Serves 6-8.

Chapter Five

THE CHASE IS ON

"And a step backward, after making a wrong turn,
is a step in the right direction."

KURT VONNEGUT
PLAYER PIANO

"Hello?"

"Make sure you're home a little early tonight. I'm taking a 6 o'clock bus to Jersey. OK?"

Unless there's an out-of-sorts trader or some other crisis at work, such as messed up data or a missing report, leaving early is not such a big deal. After all, I always log in from home. The frequency of Julia's requests to get home early enough to take the baby handoff from her or the baby sitter had increased. It seemed like her pursuit of the next esoteric cure was picking up speed.

At first, I had always inquired about the details, the reason for seeing this or that healer, their particular expertise, their training. After a while, I stopped asking, and Julia didn't seem to mind. Each disappointing encounter was kept safely away from public scrutiny.

This time, however, I could tell as soon as she walked through the door that her level of frustration with our fertility experiment had reached a tipping point.

"He asked me if we had intercourse!" Careful not to wake Ellena, she motioned toward the kitchen and repeated her report in an exasperated whisper.

"He asked me if we were having intercourse! Do you believe it? I had to take a fucking bus to New Jersey for some jerk to ask me if my husband and I knew that in order to have a child, the penis of the man needs to penetrate the vagina of the woman. At least, if you're hoping for a do-it-yourself kind of conception.

"After he asked me if we were doing it, he pressed on my sternum and kept telling me about all these people who got pregnant with his machinations. But did he say what exactly they did to have their miracle babies? Did they eat a rare mushroom marinated in post-orgasmic cervical fluid? Did they repeat a secret mantra, strip naked and prostrate themselves in front of their favorite deity? Nope. He couldn't transmit any further details. Except that all of them must've taken a refresher in the birds and the bees.

"Oh, and this is the best part," Julia continued, slowing down a bit. She took a breath, slid to the kitchen floor, crossed her legs and pressed on.

"I had to wait almost an hour for this transcendent wisdom to be bestowed upon me—and then, then," she repeated, her whisper rising into a soft, high-pitched exclamation, "then I was practically chased back to the bus, as if he had to get me out of the way before his poker-game buddies arrived!

"I was supposed to get a list of herbs, but his herbalist partner was also in a big hurry. She drove me to the bus stop and then behind a phone booth had me raise my arms in some sort of shamanistic-Kinesiological variant. Can you believe it? Behind the fucking phone booth she was pushing down on my arms shouting 'mugwort' and 'lemon balm.'"

She looked at me, with tears welling up. "I'm hungry."

I crouched down on the floor facing her, leaned over and rested my cheek against hers.

"We will do whatever it takes to find this baby together, okay? I don't know how, but we will. Now we can cross New Jersey off the list of possible routes. I never liked that state anyway," I said eliciting a weak smile from Julia.

"I'm guessing you wouldn't turn down a plate of *gnocchi* with poppy seeds."

Her eyes lit up. "Oh wow, you made *gnocchi*?"

"If you mean did I go to Fairway and buy a pound of *gnocchi* and then toss it, ever so gently, in some olive oil, apricot jam, poppy seeds and a touch of butter? Then yes, I did make *gnocchi*."

"Let me go scrub Jersey off my hands and put on some uncontaminated clothes."

"OK, it'll be ready when you're done."

She wrapped her arms around me, tears streaming down her cheeks. "How did I end up with a guy like you?"

"Years of suffering," I replied.

"Many, many years," she added.

The New Jersey fiasco might not have offered much beyond frustration, but it did encourage Julia's interest in healing herbs.

Herbal Infusion

Nettle is a popular hormone balancing herb for men and women.
Milky Oat Top strengthens the nervous system.
Tulsi is known as a stress reliever.

⅓ cup crushed **Nettle Leaves** (about ⅓ oz)
⅓ cup **Milky Oat Tops** (about ⅓ oz)
pinch **Tulsi (Holy Basil)**

Take a clean, large glass jar, such as a 2 quart-size bell jar, and add all the herbs.

Make sure to warm up the jar with some hot water before filling the jar with boiling water, so as to not shatter the glass.

Allow the water to cool down a bit before tightening the lid and steep for at least 4, but preferably 8 hours.

An easy way to strain the infusion is to rest a small strainer on top of a wide-mouth funnel.

After straining, squeeze out the remaining liquid from the pulp.

Chapter Six

SNAKE OIL AND OLIVE OIL

"One of the very nicest things about life is the way we must regularly stop whatever it is we are doing and devote our attention to eating."

LUCIANO PAVAROTTI

The sound of deliberate banging echoed through the hallway, increasing in volume as I neared the door of our apartment.

It led me to the kitchen where I found Julia standing next to the counter, knife in one hand, an oven mitt on the other, in between thrusts and poised to resume her attack on a creature that looked like the progeny of a porcupine and a three-banded-armadillo.

"It's a *Durian*," she said, glancing in my direction. "The doctor said I should have one a week."

"What a smell!" I pronounced.

"Oh, it's a bit pungent," she replied, matter-of-factly. "Actually, a woman on the subway noticed it; then she told me that because of the smell, it's been banned from hotels and public transportation in several Southeast Asian countries."

"But honestly, I stopped noticing the smell," she added cheerfully. "I already cut a piece. The man in the store said to cut along the sections."

Undaunted as she may have been by the task at hand, my valiant wife was happy to hand the knife over to me so I could perform the rest of the autopsy.

"Dr. W. said I was cold, and *Durian* would warm me."

The smell was hard to stop noticing; it was unsettling.

Tasting food starts with your eyes. Observe the color, the shape, the brightness. Then there's the feel. What is the texture? Is it dense, soft, slimy? Whether we pick food up with a fork or by hand, we sense with our fingertips. Then there's the aroma. Is it pungent, sweet, smoky? They say the olfactory sense is the source of the deepest memories. Close your eyes and open your nostrils. Does the smell bring an image to mind?

The *Durian* was not your typical supermarket piece of produce. It had an unusual appearance and texture, resembling a spiny yellowish undersea sponge, but the smell—I don't know how I ever got it into my mouth. It was quite disturbing, like a combination of sweaty sneakers and rotting cauliflower. Julia, however, was undeterred as she sat with an occasional furtive glance in my direction, chewing cube after cube of the stuff. She was literally willing to try anything to produce our elusive child.

Fortunately, there were no objections when I suggested wrapping the remaining fruit in as many plastic bags as we could find and removing it from the premises before causing any unforeseen harm to Ellena's sensitive digestive system.

I soon realized that neither plastic bags nor distance could remove the offensive odor. The only solution was to replace the stench of the *Durian* with a powerful yet palatable smell. Yup, fried onions and garlic would work nicely. They would also go well with pasta—and just in time for dinner! After slicing and browning a large onion, I added chopped garlic and continued cooking long enough to fill the air with something more reminiscent of an Italian street fair than a high school locker room.

I stirred in a jar of tomato sauce and reached for the spices. Still musing over the image of the porcupine-armadillo and my wife's non-negotiable pursuit of a miracle cure, I suddenly found myself staring at a mound of cayenne perched on top of the sauce. Quickly grabbing a spoon and carefully skimming it off, I wished I had been more diligent about following my own golden rule. The one I have been heard saying over and over. "You can always add more, but you can't take away."

My desire to study the culinary arts came almost as much as a surprise to me as to my friends and family.

Although I was the designated cook in my college house, it wasn't until I met a graduate of the Culinary Institute of America, otherwise known as the other CIA, that I developed the romantic notion of becoming a professional chef.

I do have fond memories in the kitchen helping my mom with pancakes, my dad with waffles (his only other culinary responsibility was, of course, carving the Thanksgiving turkey.) There was cake baking, using ingredients from a Betty Crocker box, in which my two jobs were turning on the mixer and licking the blades clean. I loved watching my mother make my favorite dish, Chinese style pepper steak, carefully prepared following a frayed, yellowing recipe cut from the New York Times which had been scotch-taped into the last page of *The Settlement Cookbook*. The book was the main culinary guide in our kitchen and as the cover's subtitle proclaimed, "The Way to a Man's Heart."

Inspiration for my first solo cooking project came from a family visit to the annual Little Italy street festival, The Feast of San Gennaro. Sausages with fried onions and peppers wasn't really that hard to prepare, using store-bought sausages, of course. Our apartment smelled like Mulberry Street for several days. After that, I attempted scrambled eggs and bacon, which blossomed into western omelets. I will also never forget our family's attempt to make bagels. Dad was infuriated about the price rising from 5 to 7 cents, so he decided to make them himself, with our help of course. "How hard could it be?" he asked. As it turned out—too hard to eat. Afterward Dad turned his anger in other directions, and never uttered another complaint about the price of bagels.

In college my interest in cooking turned into a passion. When I moved out of the dorm into an apartment, meal preparation became a necessity. My first apartment mate, Rich, who had left the dorm and the meal plan a year earlier for the freedom of off-campus living, was the first to show me the ropes. His approach was to stock up on lots of cans: soups, vegetables, tomato sauce and boxes of pasta. Cream of mushroom soup worked well with chicken. Macaroni and cheese wasn't too hard to make. Canned vegetables: just open, heat and serve. The truth is, I still think back fondly on those canned peas.

It wasn't long before I got the hang of it and started to do more and more of the cooking for the household, which consisted of four hungry young men. Tuna casserole was the beginning. Baked ziti, spinach lasagna and eggplant parmesan followed close behind. I went to Chinatown to buy a five-dollar-wok so I could do stir fried veggies the right way. Cooking became my college "sport." I liked it, my roommates liked it, and I never had to do the dishes.

One day, hitchhiking back to school from a weekend in New York, I got a ride from a recent graduate of the CIA. He was in the process of getting his midshipman's license, and applying for a job on a cruise ship, with the goal of cooking his way around the world. Wow, I was in awe! Sitting next to him in the car, a soon-to-be college grad with a degree in philosophy, I suddenly felt giddy realizing I could turn my love of cooking into a career and an adventure. The CIA was only a few hours' drive from Binghamton, and within a week I had visited the school.

Set in a former Jesuit novitiate in Hyde Park, New York, the CIA calls itself "The World's Premier Culinary College." Young students walk through the halls in resplendent white uniforms, proud as new Navy cadets. I toured the many kitchens where chef instructors lectured on the proper amount of celery in a *mirepoix*, and how long to let the puff pastry sit in between rolling and folding, and how to gently strain a consommé, among other crucial culinary know-how. I was sold even before seeing a class on the lawn with ice picks and chain saws creating ice sculptures for the mid-session banquet. The following week my application for an associate's degree in the Culinary Arts was in the mail.

Le Restaurant du Pavillon de France was the place to eat at the 1939 New York World's Fair. Two years later the chef and manager opened what would become the definitive French restaurant in the United States, Le Pavillon. Before it closed in 1971, chefs, cooks and waiters who trained at Le Pavillon went on to open some of New York's most famous restaurants. Lutèce, La Côte Basque, La Grenouille and La Caravelle carried the classical French tradition of artery-clogging sauces well into the 90's. On my first day at the Culinary Institute of America, we were shown a film titled The French Lunch. Shot in the kitchen of the New York landmark, La Caravelle during a lunch service, it portrayed a hectic, fast-paced, high-adrenaline experience.

As it turned out, La Caravelle is where I landed my first job after graduation.

I was hired as the *entremetier*, which literally translates as "between positions" but is actually the "vegetable cook." I was one of three on the line. The other two were the *saucier* and the *poisonnier*. The *saucier*, or sauté cook, prepared sauces and stocks during the day, and sautéed and roasted various cuts of meat at dinner. The *poisonnier* was the fish cook. He prepared the sauces for the fish dishes during the day and did the broiling and sautéing of the seafood during the dinner service. I mostly concerned myself with vegetables. During the day, I sliced, diced and turned them—turned as in *tournée* or *tournage de légumes*—hundreds of pounds of carrots, turnips and potatoes painstakingly shaped into little footballs. Why? It's just something that was, is, and will always be the perfect accompaniment to a veal chop. Besides, everyone knows that turnips look and taste better sautéed in butter and shaped like miniature pigskins.

I also made the soup du jour: cream of broccoli, cream sorrel, cream carrot, potato leek. All of these soups were made with chicken stock and, of course, plenty of cream. During dinner service, I served the vegetable of the day, various accompanying side dishes and assorted other items that had not been on the menu since 1974, but were still ordered by the regular old-timers, such as Blanquette de Veau and La Poularde Poêlée Normande.

The three of us were the first All-American cooking line in the restaurant's history. La Caravelle had always been a bastion of classical French cuisine cooked by French chefs, and Americans were only just breaking in—maybe because visas were becoming a bit harder to come by.

The French Lunch film did not adequately prepare me for the mad pace of the job. The frantic energy was more like a Marine Corps boot camp during a battle simulation: the chef calling the food orders in French mingled with furious shouting and insults hurled at waiters, dishwashers, cooks and, of course, me. I witnessed my first week of work through a haze of blurred activity. I left each night worrying that cooking was perhaps the wrong career choice.

It took a few more days for me to separate the information I needed from all the noise.

Thankfully, after a few weeks I was actually becoming comfortable, getting my work done in a timely fashion and rarely getting yelled at. In fact, as long as you're well-prepared, the backstage frenzy is exhilarating. Orders are flying in as you manage six pans on the stove. Your adrenaline is flowing. You're in the zone. Afterward you feel like you just won a boxing match.

Except of course, for the times when you haven't prepped enough, and you're in no shape to handle a rush. Then, as we insiders say, you're "in the shit."

Every night before the dinner service, Chef André would work his way down the line tasting all the sauces and soups. On one particular evening, I watched his approach with trepidation. I had over-salted the Potage Cultivateur. Not only had I messed up, but I hadn't told anyone. Dreading the repercussions of my crime, I stood silent as the Chef began his nightly ritual, proceeding down the steam-table from the Buerre Blanc to the Sauce au Poivre and finally to my station. After tasting my soup, instead of the tirade I both expected and deserved, he added his usual nightly contribution: a few twists of fresh black pepper and a little salt. The Chef gazed at me quizzically as I could not contain an audible sigh of relief.

Luckily Chef André was a heavy smoker. In fact, it was unusual for European chefs not to be. Smoking was as much a part of their culture as French bread and red wine. Fortunately for their craft, their customers shared their palate-numbing smoking habit.

As potent as that lesson was, it wasn't the last time I over-seasoned, over-salted or over-something'd a dish. That moment of panic after you've poured four ounces of pepper into a bisque is unforgettable. Sometimes I'm alert enough to scoop up most of the excess; other times all I can do is watch it quickly sink out of sight.

Since Chef Andre was the last one to touch the vegetable soup, I was technically off the hook. In my own kitchen, however, there's no one to take the blame. So, what does one do? Adding water is an option. Adding broth is better, which is why it's smart to keep some in the freezer. Also, over-seasoning can be a glorious opportunity to head in new culinary directions using the mostly unusable dish as the basis for an inventive new entrée.

Whether one is a *chef de partie* in a cutting edge, haute cuisine establishment, or a rookie cook grilling in your backyard, you better make sure that the lid is on tight before a shake of the spice jar ruins your meal.

When I stepped off the elevator, I could feel my muscles tense as the smell hit me. What now? I asked myself. Although I was pretty sure of the source of the pungent aroma, opening my apartment door confirmed my suspicions. Julia was hard at work. I found her yet again in the kitchen, presiding over a large boiling pot of soup.

"I was in Chinatown today to see Audrey's herbalist. He gave me this bag of herbs to improve my Qi. He said it's important to cook the herbs with chicken. It will enhance the herbs' potency. 'Tonify' is the word he used. 'Tonification' is needed when the Qi or blood or both are deficient."

"Quite the smell. What's in it?" I asked, turning down the flame on the boiling soup.

"Just the herbs and a cut-up chicken. Here…" She handed me the herb packet, half-filled with sticks and bark.

This was not Grandma's chicken soup.

Julia had been doing a lot of reading. She was especially drawn to the bookshelves at Health Nuts, our local health food store. There were the books promoting healthier living through good nutrition. After all, Chinese healers tended to have some special food or supplement designed to improve health in various ways. Traditional Chinese medicine, or Zhōngyi, is an ancient system using herbs, diet, acupuncture, massage, and exercise to restore health. It's helped the Chinese for 2500 years, and now it was (hopefully) helping us. It made perfect sense that changing one's diet might very well improve overall health. That packet of awful-smelling plant residue just might tip the scale in our favor.

One common theme in many approaches to better eating was a simplified diet. There was no time to waste on empty calories. It made sense to eat foods that were nutrient rich, and Julia figured that if she lightened the load on her digestive system, her body would have more energy for reproduction.

Another theme she encountered was the idea of the potential harm of unwise food combinations. For example the notion that eating too many different types of foods in one sitting can place undue stress on the digestive system. Fruit is quick to digest but, when combined with other foods, may ferment. Fermentation in the stomach can cause poor assimilation of nutrients and create excess sugar, feeding pathogenic yeast like candida.

Some of the diet gurus were advocating eating only fruit for breakfast in order to make sure your body took care of the workload of the previous day before taking on a new assignment. Especially during the initial cleansing stage of our experiments with food, we took this a step further and often ate nothing but fruit until lunch.

Julia did not believe in testing the water with one toe; she was all in. Within days, the lattes and croissants were a thing of the past. It was easy for her.

For me, changes came a bit more slowly. I was also committed but needed time to adjust. After all, my diet didn't really need to change, did it? Was it really necessary for me to give up café con leche and blueberry muffins in the morning?

But I couldn't just sit by and watch. I wanted this baby, too, and I needed to do more than just cheer Julia on. I had to stand shoulder-to-shoulder with her in the trenches.

My first food change was to adapt recipes. We had eaten lots of veggies before, but we grew more conscious of their nutritional content. Dark leafy greens, including chard, kale and spinach, were at the top of the list. They are a good source of folic acid, calcium, vitamins A, B and C, and a number of minerals. We added millet to our regular brown rice and pasta rotation. Tempeh became our go-to protein.

The next step was reducing our dairy consumption. No more cream in the carrot bisque, no more Parmesan cheese, no more yogurt sauce and no more cappuccinos. (Well maybe every now and then.) As each week passed, it got a little easier to walk by the Dunkin Donuts without sighing.

Julia's demeanor changed. She was bright-eyed, engaged, and her energy was up. After a few weeks, I too was eating mostly fruit till lunch. I brought in bags of apples, pears, berries and bananas to my cubicle. No bagels or muffins or toast and coffee. It felt good—righteous, even. We were becoming actively engaged in figuring out what worked and what didn't, rather than sitting around waiting for the next doctor's appointment.

It was about four weeks into our new regimen that I noticed I was having less stomach discomfort. I had learned in college that standing on my head was a good way to relieve gas pain. It was a technique I'd used since then, almost on a weekly basis, but a month had passed since my last headstand—it was no longer necessary. Wow, something was working!

I became an anti-dairy crusader at work, attempting to convince all within earshot to forgo the milk in their coffee. I came armed with literature on how the human digestive system was not designed to efficiently process bovine mammary production. "If you must use milk, use goat milk," I advised as my coworkers nodded, amused but rarely ready to emulate my new eating habits. Who could blame them? As far as I knew, none of the folks around me were looking to beat what all the experts said were unbeatable odds.

Vegetable Soup

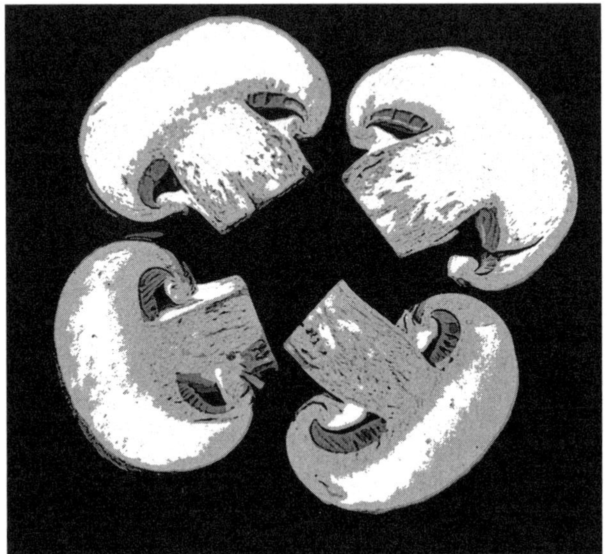

Start with plenty of onions, add the vegetables in order of firmness. Potatoes take longer than cauliflower to cook.

Onions, celery, and carrots, otherwise known as a mirepoix, is the foundation of all classical French soups and stocks. Add some garlic and almost anything else you want and you've got a soup. Vegetable soup is a great way to clean out the fridge.

When adding broccoli, I suggest doing it 2-3 minutes before serving, as it cooks quite quickly.

2 large **Onions** - ¼" dice (6 cups)
1-2 Stalks **Celery** - ⅛" dice (1 cup)
8 oz **Mushrooms** - quartered - ½" dice (3 cups)
2-3 med-large **Carrots** - ½" dice (2 cups)
3 med **Red Potatoes** - ½" dice (3 cups)
½ small head **Cauliflower** - thumb-sized pieces (3 cups)
10 -20 leaves **Chard** or **Kale or Both** - 1" dice (8 -10 cups)
2 tsps **Garlic** - minced
1 tsp **Olive Oil**
1 tsp **Salt**
½ tsp **Black Pepper**
1 tsp **Soy Sauce/Tamari** (optional)
8 Cups **Water**

In a large pot sweat Onions (see page 201.)

Add Celery and half the Garlic when Onions turn translucent, then cook another 3 minutes with occasional stirring.

Add Mushrooms and cook another 5 minutes, continue stirring.

Add Water, Carrots and Potatoes, bring to a boil and then simmer for 10 minutes.

Add Cauliflower, return to a boil then simmer another 15 minutes.

Add Greens, and continue simmering another 5 minutes.

Season with Salt and finish with Soy Sauce (optional) to taste.

Adjust the quantities of the various ingredients to taste.

Makes 4 quarts.

Chapter Seven

AUNT BEA

THE MONSTER IS COMING

*"Not everything that can be counted counts,
and not everything that counts can be counted."*

WILLIAM BRUCE CAMERON

"After 40 comes a sharp decline in ovarian reserves and not a whole lot we can do about it," so said the latest specialist. This was becoming a familiar prognosis. Several months had passed since our initial appointment, and we had less and less hope that the next expert would fix us, be they mainstream or alternative practitioners. Each time one of the experts would cite a study on advanced maternal age, Julia would say, "I have to keep as far away as I can from these statisticians."

The irony of the selective respect for the mind-body connection had become clear to her. "All this talk about how the mind affects the body, I have no doubt whatsoever that I've got a few things to straighten out in my mind. I didn't spend a quarter of a century on the couch without seeing how I can drive myself crazy and what it does to my body.

"But what about the mind body connection they keep referring to? What about all these women who keep being told it's over the minute they turn this or that age? Aren't their bodies in the room listening when somebody in a white coat shoves a stack of discouraging statistics in their face?

"Is it any surprise that the outcome of their treatments validates their theories? Can't you see how fucked up that is?"

I nodded in agreement, but part of me couldn't help but wonder: what if the experts were right? Maybe I should have payed attention to Aunt Bea when she warned me about marrying an older woman.

My great Aunt Bea was one of four sisters and three brothers who arrived at Ellis Island in steerage from Lithuania in 1907. She is my mother's father's sister, and like two of her own sisters was single all her life. Aunt Bea was a career woman with a connecting office to the President of the Acme Fast Freight Company. She hit the glass ceiling when it was knee high. Her blue-chip investments in the likes of General Electric, American Standard Oil and General Motors allowed her to live quite comfortably in a one-bedroom apartment on Central Park West overlooking the reservoir. She even had a subscription to the Metropolitan Opera.

After my mother died, I inherited Bea. At the time, she was a compact, wiry 83-year-old. Living only fifteen blocks away, I became her personal assistant, running occasional errands to the bank, post office or supermarket. She would invariably greet me with an ironic smile, a raspy voice and a remark such as: "What were you thinking when you bought that shirt?"

A conversation with Bea was like a math test you knew you were sure to flunk. The more I got to know her, the more I understood why she had never married. Over time, I became more involved in managing her finances and more accustomed to her frank, lightly abusive tone. Eventually it became clear that her savings wouldn't last, so I contacted several lawyers and embarked on a journey through the bureaucratic maze of Medicaid. Eighteen months later she had live-in care and enough money in trust to live out her life in her own home.

Aunt Bea did have a taste for life's finer things: skiing in Sun Valley, the opera, gourmet food. Even before I had officially adopted her, she paid a visit to The Gardenia Club, a restaurant overlooking a health club swimming pool on the West Side where I had my first head chef job. She became even more interested when I began my career as an entrepreneur and, being a sprightly 85, casually announced on one of my visits that she would soon drop by my restaurant, Current. I filed this threat away, hoping I wouldn't have to deal with one of the world's most demanding patrons. Then one day she called to announce that I should make her a reservation for 7:00 PM that evening.

She arrived at 6:57 with a neighbor and a friend. She ordered the always-safe, grilled salmon, plus a green salad, then finished the meal with a crème brûlée and some coffee. Her stern expression on their way out revealed little about what she thought of the meal, and although her friends raved about their experience, Bea left without saying much. I decided to take that as a good sign. Either way I was happy to see her go.

I had almost forgotten about my great aunt's visit when two days later a typically to-the-point, acerbic letter from Bea arrived, scolding me for her less-than-stellar experience. Her complaints: she was not greeted at the door by a hostess, we didn't serve Chateau d'Yquem (a sweet dessert wine) with her meal, and most seriously, the butter patties at the table were not individually wrapped. She went on to say that she would, at a later time, be returning to check on our progress. Not knowing when that might be, I decided to act quickly. The next day I went to the liquor store and bought their cheapest bottle of Chateau d'Yquem. Considering that there were bottles for $800, a $50 half-bottle seemed like a bargain. In the ensuing weeks, I made a point to stop for breakfast at my local diner and pocket all the extra butter packets. And as for the hostess—we would just have to wing it when the time came.

It was two months later when another letter announced Bea's return visit to Current. This time I was ready. I chilled the Sauterne, asked our office manager to stay late to greet our guests and got the butter packets ready. My reward was a hint of a smile and no snarky note.

I was one of the few members of the extended family who maintained an active relationship with the imperious Aunt Bea. She was always curious about both my professional and personal life. As crazy as it might seem, on a couple of occasions I brought a female friend along for a visit. Aunt Bea was always quite congenial but would not shy away from requesting a full resume, including alma mater, grade point average, employment history and other credentials. Marrying into the distinguished Sadowsky clan was no small matter.

Shortly after I met Julia, Aunt Bea must have sensed something was up because she asked about my current dating situation. I told her I'd met a nice woman. Unsurprisingly she started her usual questioning.

She was pleased to hear about Julia's European roots.

"Czechoslovakia? I was in Prague years ago, stayed in a castle. What a majestic city it is! How many languages did you say she speaks? That's remarkable. That's one thing I regret, never having learned French." After a slight pause Bea continued with a straightforward question, "And how old is she?"

"Thirty-eight," I responded, and immediately realized from her expression that I'd made a grave mistake. The congenial tone of curiosity was gone. Instead, she changed the subject and soon signaled that it was time for my departure.

Ugh, I thought on the way home. Why didn't I just say, "She's my age" or "Thirty," or not answered at all?

Bea's thoughts about my new girlfriend came, as usual, in a letter. She was certain that Julia's age would prevent us from having a family. Not having any children herself, she was particularly sensitive to this deprivation. Julia was tainted goods, past her prime; the only solution was to break off with her as soon as possible.

Julia and I read the note in shocked half-amusement. I filed it away in my "Instructions-for-Life Letters from Aunt Bea" folder.

Now here I was, four years later wondering if I would have been better off if I had listened to Aunt Bea. Then I had a second realization: I was angry. Yes, it all sounded so nice, trying new options, improving our diets, appreciating the child we already had. Yet I was also pissed. It was Julia's fault! She had duped me into marrying her. How was I to know? I'm not a woman; I don't have to worry about the state of my egg reserve. She should have told me age can be a problem. That was her responsibility.

Aunt Bea's apartment was a few too many blocks off our regular path, but when I was nearby with Ellena I would try to pop in for a visit. I got to see a side of her she hid from the world: an adoring godmother.

It was a muggy Sunday in July when we stopped off at one of my favorite playgrounds on the way to Bea's. A sprinkler fountain led to a long channel running through a giant sand box. The water flowed like a river into a large pool at the other end of the enclosure. I watched as the boy standing next to Ellena was approached by his big sister. She took his hand and led him through the water to the larger pool. Ellena had no hand to hold.

On the way home, she fell asleep around 98th Street. I picked up my pace; naps were not to be wasted. I could get a lot done in the hour and a half before she woke up. When we got home, I left her sleeping in the stroller.

Julia was in the bathtub in no more than a puddle of water. Her sweater was still on. "I was too tired to get totally undressed," she explained. I slumped against the sink cradling my head in my hands. She was tired because she was up till 2 AM doing guided imagery and reading about wheatgrass and bovine fertility cycles. She was tired because she was a woman obsessed. She often appeared distracted, but it was really her laser focus—an ability to block out any outside interference, including me.

They say that men often marry their mothers. I married my anti-mother.

Helen Sadowsky Baum was an intelligent, rational, organized, loving, but not overly affectionate mom. I do not recall a lot of hugging. She married my father at the advanced age of 30 and struggled with his lack of motivation and lack of income and his illness and eventual death when he was just 50 and she was 48. She was strong and kept it all together. She worked as a bookkeeper. Her books were always well kept.

I have always been attracted to women who were nothing like Helen Sadowsky. Julia is emotional and extremely affectionate. Teetering towers of her books and papers were piled up on every available surface.

As we confronted our "fertility crisis," Julia lead and I followed, but the whole ordeal was exhausting me. I was tired of the Chinese herbs she made me cook that stunk up the house. I was tired of going to Massachusetts to see one more specialist. I was tired of holding my breath every 28 days until another period showed up. I was tired of Julia's tiredness and her ever-decreasing displays of affection. These days, it seemed all of her attention, aside from her search for a cure, was focused on Ellena.

Was I jealous of my daughter? Wasn't she our angel? Didn't she make this whole struggle so much easier? Yes, she did, but she was also a constant reminder that something was missing.

I could not escape them. Siblings. They were everywhere I looked. One day Ellena and I were in the 106th St. playground; she was playing with Robert and his big sister Megan. Beth, who lived across the street, was there, too, trumpeting the arrival of her new baby brother. Zak and Sam, the twins, arrived with their mother and her big fat, ready-to-pop belly. The kids were taking turns leading each other around the jungle gym. Ellena was barely keeping up. I was strategically placed to collect a toll every time they came by, a job I much preferred to sitting with the moms and dads. Who wouldn't?

As a few more children joined the parade I was keenly aware that Ellena was the only "only" child. Did she notice? Was this really for my daughter's sake that we had turned ourselves inside out?

"The monster is coming, the monster is coming," the children were screaming as they thundered down the hall in a cloud of gleeful abandon. The little ones, including Ellena, struggled to keep up but with my help safely reached the living room where they had built a fort to keep Monster Mike, this year's designated demon, at bay.

We were at Strauss House, deep in the Catskill Mountains, where for the last weekend in July our collegial gang of 20 adults and 14 kids takes over a large streamside house surrounded by hundreds of acres of forest. It's a family festival: families of a core group of friends who have known each other since grade school. It's something we look forward to all year long: escape from the city, a walk in the stream, a drowsy afternoon nap, but mostly watching and enjoying the kids run untethered through the house and fields. It's satisfying to give children three essential gifts: friendship, chaos, and safety.

Our collective was a mixed bag of two, one, and no-kid families, but it seemed like they were all expanding. I was acutely aware of being one of the single-kid units. I watched the new babies with their moms and dads and siblings hovering over them. Since the diagnosis, there had been a tape loop playing over and over in my head: I am happy with one child; my life is blessed. It was reassuring, but if it was so true, why did I have to keep repeating it?

Ellena was happily nestled in Julia's lap as they sat amongst the other mommies, and although she didn't look the part, Julia was the oldest one there. Might I have been better off with one of the other younger moms? I pictured a life with Beth playing with the dog on our suburban lawn, or maybe with Sue, driving our two or three kids in the minivan. Aunt Bea would have been so happy.

I watched as the other kids piled the couch pillows against the door. Suddenly it was clear to me that I was not ready to give up. I wanted another child.

The bumper-to-bumper traffic across the George Washington Bridge jolted me back to the hot, smelly, car-honking, real world. We weren't the only ones who got away for the weekend.

Returning to the city with the cool forests of the Catskills a hundred miles behind us was always the toughest part of weekend getaways. Were these throngs of people on West End Avenue there when we left? We unloaded the car and moved all our bags into the lobby. As Julia headed upstairs with Ellena, I drove downtown to return the rental car. After handing over the Ford Taurus to the Hertz agent, I decided to walk home from 73rd Street. The concrete sidewalks and brick buildings had not yet let go of the midday heat. I felt a mix of emotions as I walked up Broadway: annoyance with the sweltering city, delight to have escaped to an idyllic place, anguish about the endless fertility fight.

I got home to find Julia and Ellena in the bathtub. They were singing a Hungarian song about the little girl who went to the market and filled her basket with chocolate and bananas.

Keeshlany, ha kee medyen a peeyatsrah…

I stood outside the bathroom listening, and I knew we would figure this out. Just because we had lost hope in the healers didn't mean we lost hope. The woman I married might be older than the moms at Strauss house, but she was a force I couldn't and didn't wish to resist. There was no turning back for either of us.

Broccoli with Garlic and Cilantro

This one is simple, elegant, nutritious and delicious.

1 head of **Broccoli**
1 tsp minced **Garlic**
1 tsp **Olive Oil**
1 ½ Tbsp chopped **Cilantro** (including stems)
½ - 1 tsp **Soy Sauce/Tamari**
Water if necessary

Cut head of Broccoli into evenly sized florets. The stems are also quite edible, after a good peeling to remove the woody exterior. Cut them in a ½" dice.

Heat your pan, good and hot and add the chopped Garlic and Oil, stir with wooden spoon, don't let it burn.

Add Broccoli quickly when Garlic starts showing signs of color (Don't let it brown.)

Add 1 teaspoon of Water, just enough to keep the Broccoli from burning.

Add Soy Sauce. Cook 1 minute while stirring. Add chopped Cilantro. Cook another two minutes.

Add another teaspoon of Water if necessary (if it gets too dry and starts burning.)

Serves 6-8.

Chapter Eight

FIRST COUSCOUS THEN PARIS

"To travel hopefully is a better thing than to arrive."

Robert Louis Stevenson

I left work early to meet Ellena and Maya at the 84th Street Barnes and Noble. Maya had to go to class, and Julia was teaching till 9:00. I arrived just in time to a packed room of wide-eyed toddlers with their accompanying parents or nannies, gathered for a special storytelling event. Maya, a thoughtful, gentle doctoral candidate in Molecular Biology at Columbia University, had been Ellena's much loved friend and helper for the last six months. She was from South India, and aside from being a great companion for our daughter, was also a gifted cook, introducing Ellena to dhal and curry and even some spicier offerings, such as black pepper *papadams*.

At the storytelling, Ellena especially relished a chance to scream "Noooo" during the reading of one of her favorite books, "The Baby Blue Cat Who Said No." She was still beaming when we left the store and headed uptown. After sucking down the last of her juice, she fell asleep in the stroller on our way up Broadway.

I had to log into work as soon as I got home to finish some reports, so cooking was out of the question. I'd have to rely on our favorite alternate meal source, the health food store a few blocks from home. Today's special at Heath Nuts was vegetarian black bean chili and Moroccan quinoa couscous with mint and eggplant.

Julia's dietary experiments were ongoing. She continued adding ingredients to the "acceptable" list—chickpeas, millet, adzuki beans—and subtracting others. Tofu, for example, was too tough on the thyroid. As far as I knew, black beans were still OK, and although I wasn't sure about the fertility-friendliness of quinoa, the combination was appealing, and I decided to take my chances.

Actual couscous is made of crushed durum wheat semolina, unlike pasta which is made from ground semolina. It originates in North Africa. Although made from wheat, it looks like a grain, fooling most people into thinking it's a whole grain. It is typically the base for a meat and vegetable stew but can really be an accompaniment to anything.

My first encounter with couscous was in the North of France. Two months after graduating from college, outfitted with a new sleeping bag and an internal frame backpack, my girlfriend Sarah and I embarked on a post-college, rite-of-passage backpacking trip through Europe. We had been going out for a year, and had done some travelling together, including a hitchhiking trip around California. We got along well enough, and decided to take our travelling to the next level.

Armed with the budget traveler's Bible, *Let's Go Europe*, Sarah and I were keen on stretching our dollars, which meant hitchhiking whenever possible. Although our main motivation was saving money, we also wanted to see the side of life missed by the students with EuroRail passes who traveled from one capital city to the next in soundproof railroad cars.

Since both of us had travelled thousands of miles hitching rides, the notion of getting into a car with total strangers wasn't too daunting. Even if we often couldn't hold in-depth conversations with drivers due to a language barrier, it was astonishing how much one could understand with no more than a few key phrases coupled with limitless inventive gestures.

As expected, getting from London to Paris was easy, at least at first. We took the tube to the outskirts of the city and barely had time to set down our bags before a lorry stopped. It took ten minutes of conversation to realize that our driver was actually speaking English. A Welsh accent is not easy for a Brooklyn boy. Our destination was Dover, home of the White Cliffs, where we'd catch a boat across the English Channel to Calais, France, and a few hours later arrive in Paris.

The European continent lay before us rife with possibilities, like the soon-to-be-blossoming cherry trees lining the streets near the ferry slip.

As we arrived at the Dover terminal, high winds and rain on the English Channel cancelled the speedier hovercraft, leaving us with no choice but to settle down for the two hour wait for the next car ferry. Our lamentations were overheard by a young Brit, who turned to us, introduced himself as Don and offered a ride to Paris. Let's go Europe!

For a few minutes we stood on the cold, wet ferry deck watching the White Cliffs fade from view, then opted for the less rugged experience of the cabin for the rest of the ride. The gray choppy waves eventually carried us to the dimly lit shoreline of Calais.

We joined Don, who was in his car ready to debark. Moments later we touched down on French soil, and I felt as though I had suddenly stepped into a dream I had dreamt many times, with the mellifluous sounds of the sexiest language in the world streaming from every direction; billboards with words that evoked a memory of my French high school teacher, Monsieur Mayorkas, and his perplexing cue cards. With wide open eyes, I feasted on the verdant countryside of rural farmland and farming communities as we drove through the small villages, staying clear of the Autobahn.

We'd been on the road for less than an hour when Don pulled into a gas station, lifted the hood of the car and announced cheerfully that due to a small leak in the radiator, we would need to make occasional pit stops to rehydrate.

After the third stop in less than an hour, Don appeared to be losing patience. He returned to the car carrying more than the usual jug of water. Out of a small plastic bag he pulled a package of crackers and a half-dozen eggs. Enjoying the slightly salty crackers, Sarah and I watched Don lift the hood and pour the water into the radiator:

"My mate Fred in Yorkshire told me about cracking an egg into the radiator to stop a leak," Don said, opening the carton of eggs. "It's supposed to congeal and plug up the hole."

Sarah and I nodded in agreement as he proceeded to crack the first egg.

"Do you think you should beat them first, like for an omelet?" I asked, wondering if my culinary leanings could come in handy here.

"Nah, he didn't say anything about beating them, although I could go for a nice omelet with a side of bacon." We watched Don crack in two more eggs.

"Do you think you need them all?" Sarah asked, as he reached for the last two.

"Might as well!"

He closed the hood and off we went.

Everything seemed fine for about 20 minutes, until smoke started seeping out of the air vents with an odor reminiscent of a Greek diner. The car slowed despite Don's best effort to coax it onward, and we coasted to a stop in a gravel parking lot next to a 200-year-old tavern.

Welcome to France!

It wasn't hard to recognize true providence, so without further discussion we left the smoking car and went inside.

A real French country tavern: slate roof, thick ceiling beams and exposed brick walls. The place smelled of age and tarragon. There was a long bar on the left and eight tables to the right. We were apparently the night's first customers; the place was empty. A waiter appeared, greeting us with a big smile and a few words in French, of course. I guess I shouldn't have been surprised when Don responded in kind, and we headed for a table by the window followed by the waiter with three menus and three glasses of water. I could make little sense of the menu, and Don wasn't a big help. (Sarah had taken four years of Spanish.) I was nervous as the waiter returned to take our order. I could feel my middle and high school French teachers pulling up chairs beside us as the waiter turned to me first and asked, "What can I get you?" In perfect English. Turned out he was from Manchester.

Don ordered red wine and charcuterie: pâté, sausages, cheeses and bread. Two hours later he was undeterred by our objections to ordering more wine due to our limited budget—so Bruce the waiter happily kept our glasses full. I was sure I'd read a paragraph about just such an experience in *Let's Go*. Wasn't this the part where they'd whack us on the side of the head and steal our passports?

After a couple of hours, Don decided that we needed something other than pâté, cheese, bread and wine, although I was doing just fine with those four items. At this point, Bruce came over to sit with us and suggested the couscous, a Moroccan lamb and vegetable stew served over the tiny grain-like semolina infused with mint and cayenne. "Sure, why not?" I replied. At this point I was open to all suggestions and, come to think of it, was a little hungry. The couscous was good—I mean really good—tender chunks of stewed lamb with large helpings of carrots, turnips and potatoes in a surprisingly light broth, perfectly balanced between mint and spice. My first meal in France surpassed all my expectations.

Many hours and even more wine later, we were served coffee and a glass of cognac. It must have been the good stuff, because it caused quite a stir when we dumped it in our coffee. Fortunately, as uncultured Americans we were given a pass. It was a memorable cup of coffee.

As the discussion turned towards plum and apricot tarts, we were joined by another Brit, a white haired, elegantly dressed, potbellied man in his 60's. Mr. Floyd was obviously a regular customer, as Bruce knew just what to bring him, and of course another bottle of Bordeaux was opened. Mr. Floyd was a retired English gentleman who was living on an old farm nearby. He told us about his recently finished renovations, and his plans to convert his barn into a disco.

He invited us all to spend the night at his place, and since we were clearly not in any shape to hit the road, we accepted. Sarah, Don, Bruce the waiter, Mr. Floyd and I squeezed into a sleek black Mercedes and headed off into the darkness. The buildings we could see on Mr. Floyd's estate were pretty run down, but the renovated living space had a rustic elegance. In the living room, two perpendicular couches—one magenta, one green—dominated the oak floor. Mr. Floyd begged us to sit, and proceeded to bring out several top shelf bottles: Armagnac, Calvados, a Bordeaux and two single malts. As if we hadn't been drinking for the last four hours!

I was far too gone to partake in any more libations; with drooping eyelids, I joined Sarah, curled up on her sleeping bag in the far corner of the room. With Bruce passed out on the couch and Don and Mr. Floyd refilling their glasses, I drifted off to sleep.

The next thing I remember is waking up in a dreamlike haze to the sound of Mr. Floyd's insistent voice repeating over and over: "Come now, mate, what on earth are you doing on that bloody couch, when the bed is so much more pleasant? Come now, come…"

Don was not budging from the couch, and Mr. Floyd was becoming more shrill. It seemed to go on for hours. The cajoling turned into shouting about "ungrateful guests" and "never opening one's home to strangers."

Eventually, the ruckus gave way to a peaceful silence.

In the morning, while the others slept, Sarah and I headed outside to let the country air purge some of the night's excesses. We circled a small pond, chatting about the chaos of the previous night. "If we continue living like this, our money won't last two weeks!" I remarked.

"And neither will our livers," said Sarah with a half laugh.

Eventually Bruce made his way outside to inform us that Mr. Floyd was not particularly keen on driving us anywhere. It was a beautiful three-mile walk on picturesque country roads back to the restaurant and the car and the rest of our gear.

Walking may well be the best cure for a hangover.

As we said our goodbyes, I handed Don half of our francs—the equivalent of about twenty dollars. I could tell he was not entirely pleased with the exchange, but he didn't chide us.

Sarah and I collected our bags, headed back onto the road and stuck out our thumbs. The last thing we saw as we leaped into the back of a small white Peugeot was Don holding up an old radiator he'd rummaged from a junk pile behind the restaurant.

Couscous, even when it's really quinoa, reminds me of my very first night in France.

Quinoa and Cold Cucumber Tabouli

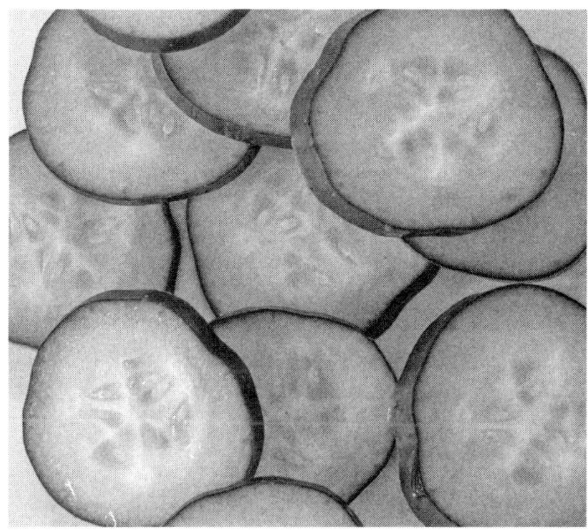

I really like the warm and silky quinoa combined with the cool and crunchy cucumbers. It's got that Yin-Yang thing going on. As a variation try using short grain brown rice instead of quinoa.

1 cup **Quinoa**
1 ⅔ cups **Water**
1 med **Cucumber** - ⅛" dice (2 cups)
1 ½ tsps **Oil** from **Garlic infusion**
2 Tbsp chopped **Parsley**
1 tsp **Soy Sauce/Tamari**

Rinse Quinoa well, and add to pot with Water and ½ teaspoon of Garlic Oil.

Bring to boil and then simmer for 15 minutes.

Combine Cucumber, remaining Garlic Oil, Parsley and Soy in a small bowl and leave refrigerated.

When Quinoa is cooked stir in cucumber mixture.

Add Salt or Hot Sauce if desired.

Serves 6-8.

Chapter Nine

SUCH A BRAVE BOY

"I believe that what we become depends on what our fathers teach us at odd moments, when they aren't trying to teach us."

UMBERTO ECO
FOUCAULT'S PENDULUM

"What's going on?" Julia asked as I was brushing my teeth after putting Ellena in her crib.

I turned away from her and shrugged.

"You haven't been saying much the last few days," she observed.

It was hard for me to look at her. It had been three days since her period came.

"You're mad, of course you're mad; it's okay for you to be angry at me, but I think I'd rather have you yell than give me the silent treatment."

I've always been good at the silent treatment. In fact, it's my specialty.

"I'm disappointed too," she continued. "I want to give you this baby. I do. I really feel I need to have this child for you and for Ellena, and I'm ready to turn myself inside out. I don't know what else I can do..."

I could tell that tears were imminent; still I couldn't help but snap back. "Would you stop saying you're doing it for me? Don't do it for me; do it for you." I turned to leave the room but she grabbed my arm pulling me toward her.

"I can't do it for me," she said, tears streaming down her cheeks. "I don't even know who I am anymore; how can I do it for me?"

Of course she was right. There were sacrifices I, too, was ready to make for either of my girls which I would never do just for myself. Giving up my three daily cups of coffee was easy knowing it was for them.

"I guess we're both in the same boat," I said, as she pulled me closer still. "We both need someone to do everything for. I'm sorry," I continued. "I don't do angry well." But I still doubted she really wanted me to start yelling. The last thing I needed was to turn into my father.

My father never hit me, but his rage was palpable. You could see it in his face gathering force, ready to explode. You could even see the anger move down his neck and into his arms.

Bernard Baum was born in 1917 to second generation Polish and Russian immigrants. His father was a travelling salesman. Bernie grew up in Williamsburg, Brooklyn, the oldest of five children. In 1938 he beat out doctors, lawyers and engineers for a coveted job in the Depression-era post office, only to quit after a few months, bored by the routine. He tried many careers, including his paternal model: sales. He never found a satisfying role in this world.

I only knew him as a roofer, a line of work he got into with help from his father-in-law. On rainy days, the phone wouldn't stop ringing. My uncles often said Dad was the smartest one in the family. They were both well-off businessmen, and to me their praise carried an air of condescension.

With his sand-colored hair and gray-blue eyes, Bernard Baum could have been a handsome man, but his pleasant features were eclipsed by a look of chronic frustration, as if he had misplaced something he urgently needed: his wallet or car keys, perhaps.

I know that my father loved me and was proud of my achievements. He was pleased to have a son smart enough to have skipped third grade with a decent jump shot to boot. For many men of his generation, having a son was far more validating than having a daughter. My uncle Irwin recalls being with my Dad in the hospital waiting room as my father paced back and forth waiting for his wife to give birth to their first child.

"If it's a boy," said my father, "it's Chinese food on me!"

My sister was born on November 15, 1953 at 5:00 PM, a perfect time for dinner. But there was no Chinese food.

During summer vacations, staying at my grandparents' house in the Catskills, my sister and I would wait at the bottom of the road on Friday evenings for Dad's arrival from the City. I knew there would always be fresh onion rolls from the bakery on Saturday and Sunday which we'd eat together while reading the newspaper. He taught me to lift up the paper and funnel all the crumbs into my mouth when I was done. If I had trouble falling asleep in the evenings, he'd scratch my back as I lay on my bed until I drifted off to dreamland.

He drove me to Bensonhurst Brooklyn to buy my first drum set from a personal ad in Brooklyn Buy Lines. Allowing a drum set in a small apartment—what better proof of his affection could there be?

Dad lived through the Depression, World War II and, just barely, my bar mitzvah in 1969, dying two weeks later. He had been sick for several years before his death: diabetes, high blood pressure, gout, polycythemia. He took enough medication to keep our corner pharmacy in business. I didn't realize it at the time, but he must've been in a lot of pain. I don't think I ever knew a healthy non-medicated father. Perhaps that explains his temper. It didn't take much to set him off.

In 1968 my parents sent me and my sister Amy to a Jewish Federation summer camp in Surprise Lake, New York. We were signed up for the last two of the summer's three sessions, with a weekend at home in between. Amy convinced me to take all our belongings with us on the break in the hopes of talking our parents into letting us stay home. She hated camp, and she was skilled at using me as her pawn. With her encouragement, I wrote home letters with drawings of me behind bars, begging to be released. Dad came to meet us at the bus, saw all our luggage and started screaming.

We should've left it at camp! What if he hadn't brought his car? He roared, creating a humiliating scene. On the way home, we stopped at an Italian deli in the Bronx to buy some sandwiches. He sent us in alone as he parked the car. Amy got a plain ham sandwich; I ordered salami with mustard. When my father arrived, still simmering from the luggage betrayal, he looked at our sandwiches and exploded. Apparently, this was not what you order at the most famous hero shop in the Bronx. Where were all the fixings? The brunt of his wrath was directed at my sister and her plain ham sandwich. I was spared; I got mustard.

Then there was a trip my father, sister and I took to our grandmother's apartment. Upon arriving home my mother asked her how it went. Amy, quoting my father, replied, "It was okay until the sonofabitch cut us off." Years later my mother taped a "Dennis the Menace" cartoon above her desk. Dennis was riding in a car with his parents and the caption read: "When are you going to learn me how to drive? I know all the words." Riding in a car with Dad was a noncredit course in Brooklyn profanity.

My Uncle Irwin tells a story of our families vacationing together at a Catskills hotel. My cousin Stanley and I went into Irwin's room to ask him for some change to play pinball. Irwin was lying on the bed, attempting to take his afternoon nap, and we were standing at the door not so quietly discussing our options. Do we wake him or tip-toe away? My uncle suddenly sat up in the bed and started yelling at us to leave. I turned to Stanley and said, "Ask him now; he's in a good mood."

"I couldn't help but wonder what life was like at your house," my uncle would say, as he recounted the incident.

Not long after that episode, Irwin and the rest of the relatives had a chance to witness the goings-on at my house. It was a Thanksgiving gathering, and after everyone had arrived, my mother insisted I change into my new wool pants. They itched; I refused. A lot of screaming ensued as my mother dragged me into the bedroom. We compromised on a less itchy pair, but when I came back to the table I found that my sister had taken my spot next to Grandma. More screaming followed, then out of the corner of my tear-soaked eye I saw my father pick up his plate like a discus. The plate never left his hand, though for a terrifying moment I could imagine it hurtling toward me. My childhood was not infrequently punctuated by such threats. None of them were ever carried out, but that didn't stop me from living in constant fear that I was one wrong word away from disaster.

Throughout my life, I have strived to avoid turning into my father. I've been genial, not embittered; easy going, not high strung; my jobs have paid well, not meagerly. Like many of my friends who have grown up with difficult fathers, I've become my anti-father. But the "hidden father" has remained. He's always there, lurking somewhere in the dark recesses of my psyche, like a life-threatening virus that can attack when I least expect it.

Although on some level I knew he was sick, I was not prepared to lose him. Two weeks after my bar mitzvah, Dad was in the hospital again.

"When can we go and see him?" I asked my mother.

"Soon," she answered.

The next day, my friend and neighbor Henry and I walked home from school together. I remember leaning on each other as we made our way down the street. As we reached my building, my sister was outside walking our dog; her eyes were red and she wouldn't look at me. She said nothing as we rode up in the elevator. He died, I said to myself. Dad is dead. Uncle Irwin's presence in the kitchen confirmed my suspicion. He left the room, and my mother told me the news. What exactly did she say? I don't remember. I do remember going into my room. They gave me space—space to do what? I felt the weight of this tragedy, but it didn't feel like it was happening to me.

At the funeral home, I went into the bathroom and stared at the light, hoping to make myself cry, because I should have been crying. If I wept, everyone would stop telling me what a brave boy I was to stand there next to my weeping mother and sister without giving in to tears. I wanted it all to end. I was supposed to be sad. Everyone else was sad. Why couldn't I feel the same? All I knew was that I was not feeling brave.

I was not quite thirteen and my father, who had never fully been there for me, was forever gone. But his anger lingers in my body, I see his rage pressing through the corners of my lips. I must make sure to contain it, to keep myself and everyone around me safe. Julia pushed and pulled. She was right; I needed to fight more, scream more, let it out more. She advocated a controlled burn. I feared a forest fire.

Veggie Burgers

Rice, beans, oats, barley, lentils, flax seed, flour, nuts, and seeds are all possible binders for a proper veggie burger. Onions, celery, carrots, mushrooms, kale, sweet potatoes, and garlic are among an endless list of additions providing flavor, texture and color. Putting them together in the right proportions is the challenge. This recipe provides a good balance between consistency and flavor and can be used as a base for other ingredients as well; spinach or kale for example. Just make sure to cook them to a dry state. Raw veggies will release water and will make the burgers mushy.

1 large **Onion** - ¼" dice (2 cups)
3-4 stalks **Celery** - ⅛" dice (2 cups)
2 tsps **Garlic** - minced
1 ¼ tsp **Salt**
1 tsp **Black Pepper (fresh ground)**
1 cup **Cashews**
½ cup **Sunflower Seeds**
¾ cup **Rolled Oats**
1 ½ cups cooked short grain **Brown Rice**
2 cups diced **Mushrooms** (white, crimini, baby bella)

Cook Brown Rice using 1 cup Rice to 1 ½ cups Water plus 1 teaspoon Olive Oil.

In a small pot sweat Onions (see page 201.) Add Celery and Garlic and cook till dry (almost sticking) and set aside.

Cook Mushrooms in a tablespoon of Water until dry (they will release a lot of their own liquid.)

Put Cashews and Sunflower Seeds in food processor until finely ground.

Add Rolled Oats and pulse lightly until blended.

Add Rice and blend well but do not overdo it.

Remove Nuts, Oats and Rice from processor and place in a large mixing bowl.

Add Mushrooms and ⅔ of the cooked and cooled Onion-Celery-Garlic mixture to the processor and blend well, occasionally scraping down the sides.

Remove from processor and add to Nut-Oats-Rice mixture.

Add the remaining Onion-Celery-Garlic as well and blend together with a spoon.

Create equal-sized patties, place on baking tray and put in hot oven at 375 degrees for 25 minutes.

Then turn off oven and let them stay in for another 10-15 minutes.

Let cool before removing from pan. They will firm up as they cool.

Serves 6-8.

Chapter Ten

DA BOYS

"It is one of the blessings of old friends that you can afford to be stupid with them."

RALPH WALDO EMERSON
EMERSON IN HIS JOURNALS

It had been ten months since we got the lab report that had changed our lives. Ten months of doctors and clinics and more labs. Ten months of healers and shamans and mystics. Ten months of alternating hope and dejection orbiting around Julia's menstrual cycle. Ten months of worrying if my underwear was too tight. Ten months of kneeling on the floor instead of sitting at my office desk to keep my sperm cool. Ten long months.

It was March, and coinciding with the transition to warmer weather, it was time for Boys Weekend. Affectionately known as BW, it's an annual gathering of a group of guys, the core of whom have known each other since childhood in Washington Heights, New York, in the 1960's. Eighteen or so of us—lawyers, programmers, shrinks, entrepreneurs—all taking the weekend off to savor the pleasures of collective friendship. I was lucky enough to gain membership through my best friend Jeff and his college roommate. I am a relative newcomer, joining only 19 years ago.

The agenda for Boys Weekend is: music and food, then more music and more food. It is a celebration of our community and a renewal of our youthful passions. Best of all, it's a weekend away from lawyering and shrinking and programming, a weekend when children and wives and deadlines recede into the background.

This year, however, I was seriously considering missing the gathering. There was a slight hesitation in Julia's response when I reminded her that Boys Weekend was coming up.

"Oh, you should definitely go; you could really use it," she said.

"I'm not sure it's the best time..." I began, but she interrupted.

"That's crazy; you have to go; you are going," she said, walking over to me and wrapping her arm around my waist. "Don't worry about us. Elenka and I will have a swinging Girls Weekend Party!"

I went over to Ellena, who was on the floor playing with a pot and some wooden spoons. I picked her up and started to twirl her.

"But I don't want to miss a party!" I exclaimed.

Ellena was laughing as her head arched back and her eyes swept the ceiling. I wasn't one hundred percent sold on the idea of leaving my girls for three days. Weekends were the only time Julia had to herself. But it was clear she wouldn't stand for my self-sacrifice, and I could really use a break.

Now that the vote was cast, I could start planning menus.

Food has always been an important part of Boys Weekend, whether it's mushroom risotto, steamed lobsters with garlic butter, take-out Chinese food or pizza from down the block. Cooking for the Boys is truly a labor of love—plus it's a chance to relive the fun side of cooking professionally.

I have always strived to make the food a special part of the festivities, and it's been a challenge to balance my role as chef with that of participant: to cook a memorable meal and still leave plenty of time for everything else. I have a reputation to uphold, and of course at my core I want everyone to love my food and therefore, love me.

A big part of the weekend for me is being able to leave my to-do list at home, but it's not like I don't have a special Boys Weekend list: lentil soup, playing guitar, drums, bass, relaxing, an afternoon nap, hanging out with old friends. Not a bad list but a list nonetheless. The real challenge has always been to do everything on this list without feeling the need to do everything on the list.

BW floats around geographically; this year it was in Montclair, New Jersey. I chose to not get too extravagant about meal planning, so John, the host, and I decided to order take-out on Friday and make one collective home-cooked meal on Saturday. It's no fun spending half the weekend shopping and preparing food, but I didn't feel right about the Boys eating exclusively out of white take-out containers. Although I did a fair amount of the cooking at home, there's nothing like cooking for a crowd—and then, of course, basking in the glow of the blissfully well-fed.

Unlike prior years, I wanted to do some of the food prep in advance so I could arrive with some cooked ingredients and not have a ton of work during the weekend. But before I knew it, it was Thursday night, and I had, as they say in the Old Country, bupkis. Although I still didn't have a definitive plan, three heads of garlic and seven pounds of onions should give me a good start. I small-diced the onions, because that would allow for a number of options. I was thinking maybe soup or sauce or both.

Seven pounds were a lot of onions, but as I have always said, "You can't have too many onions!" I scraped them off the cutting board into a large pot, added a little salt and olive oil and heated them as I sliced more.

Julia entered the kitchen just as they started sizzling.

"Hmm, that smells good; is any of this for us?" she inquired.

"Ahh, I hadn't thought about dinner," I responded, scraping another batch into the pot. Julia stood there looking hungry.

"How about fried rice?" I asked remembering the leftover rice in the fridge from two nights before. "I might be able to spare some onions."

Before getting started on the rice, I continued dicing the rest of the onions. Three heads of garlic are a lot to peel; fortunately the cloves were pretty big. I cut off the ends and then smashed them with the flat side of the knife to make peeling easier. After that came lots of chopping. I have at times used a food processor for large quantities of garlic, but considering the cleanup required, it's not a big timesaver. After chopping, I placed a couple of tablespoons of the garlic in with the cooking onions. The rest was covered in olive oil and stored in a jar in the fridge. That was as much prep work as I was going to get to do. Bring on the Boys!

I had arranged to get a lift from Sam, who was driving from Queens. With Ellena in the stroller, Julia helped me carry all the stuff downstairs. Our daughter had a playdate at Barnes and Noble, so they couldn't hang around and wait with me.

"Don't worry about a thing, Eddie Baum," Julia announced gaily. "We are going to have a great time, and you will, too!"

As we hugged, my uncertainties surfaced again. Was this the right thing to do? Weren't we in the midst of a crisis? I was going off to play with the Boys at a time when I should really be trying to figure out the next strategy for our baby chase. I said none of this to Julia, and for some reason neither did I say that I loved her. All I could do was hold on a bit tighter and longer than usual. When we broke our grasp, I didn't look at her. I couldn't. I turned quickly to Ellena, who had been watching us, and gave her a squeeze—a really good long guilt-ridden squeeze.

They headed up the street, and when they reached the corner Julia turned to look back. I waved; she pointed Ellena in my direction, and for a moment we were all waving. Then they crossed the street and were gone.

Standing there with my guitar, bags of spinach and mushrooms, pots, bowls, knives, wires and pedals, I was on the verge of tears, which was as far as I usually get. I was already missing Ellena, feeling like a delinquent father. Thankfully, Sam pulled up before I could spiral any deeper into self-loathing. His ear-to-ear smile bore no trace of guilt over leaving his family. After a quick bro hug, he helped squeeze my bags into the back of his station wagon. A few minutes later we were in the car on the West Side Highway heading towards the George Washington Bridge. By the time I saw "WELCOME TO NEW JERSEY" my self-reproach was beginning to dissipate. I took a deep breath and leaned back against the seat. Boys Weekend had begun.

It was about an hour drive to John's and with each mile a bit more of the guilt fell away. When we arrived at our destination, it felt like a homecoming. The boys filtered in throughout the day and into the evening. Each new arrival was met with a Loyal-Order-of-Water-Buffalos-style welcome. Ours was a secret society that admitted all newcomers. First come, first serve on the sleeping spots. Beds, couches, air mattresses went quickly, leaving the late arrivers with cushions and flimsy foam pads. The downstairs bedroom was reserved for chronic snorers.

Friday night we ordered Chinese Food from a local Hunan Restaurant. Saturday breakfast was pancakes. I served as advisor to the three pancake-makers, offering suggestions only when necessary. "I'm taking orders for the 'special recipe,'" said Joseph with a meaningful nod in my direction.

"I'm okay," I answered, looking down.

Since I'd arrived, I'd passed on the beer, I'd passed on the wine, I'd passed on the joints, and now I was declining the pot pancakes. I needed to protect my seed from any damaging influence. Keep all parts of the baby making machine in tip top shape. But so far I offered no explanation about my abstinence to the Boys.

I hadn't intended on sharing my story over the weekend, but I also didn't intend not to. Charlie was sitting at the dining room table after the breakfast crowd had dispersed, sipping some coffee. I joined him.

"Did you have one of Joe's high-octane pancakes?" he asked.

"No, I've been abstaining."

"Really! Why is that?"

"I'm trying to keep my sperm healthy."

"Oh?" he said, looking at me with raised eyebrows.

"We've been trying for a while to give Ellena a sibling. The doctors have basically said that it's not going to happen. Julia's hormone levels are too high, but we're not giving up yet," I explained.

Charlie is a good listener, and not only because he's an Ivy League trained therapist. Charlie is also an only child.

"I never really thought much about not having any siblings," he mused. "I've always had lots of friends."

In fact, Charlie did have more than his share of friends. His presence, his house, the circles he moved in were the signs of a generous, compassionate, socially well-adjusted individual. Charlie has a way of turning friends into family. There were many of us that made up BW, but Charlie was the glue.

"I wasn't sure I should come this weekend. There's been a lot going on," I confessed.

"I'm glad you did," Charlie said. "It might be the best thing you did, not just for yourself, but for Julia and your daughter, taking the weekend off."

Looking at Charlie made a light bulb go off in my head. It was clear that Ellena wouldn't be so handicapped being an only child. Maybe I could start letting go of the idea that she needed a sibling. Sometimes being an only child makes a person more likely to have meaningful friendships.

"Is that the other half?" I asked, pointing to a plate with a piece of pancake. Charlie grinned and nodded.

"Got any maple syrup?" I took a tentative bite and chewed slowly. "Doesn't taste too bad," I remarked.

"I'm just starting to taste mine," he replied, opening his eyes wider.

After finishing the pancake I realized that I had, in fact, decided to take the weekend off after all. My fertility quest could wait till Monday—or maybe Tuesday.

Charlie and I were joined by a few other boys. With Miles Davis playing softly in the background, we sat together talking of bad bosses and leaky pipes. After a while we could hear the first few organ notes from "You Can't Always Get What You Want" float up from the basement—a musical invitation.

"Shall we?" Charlie asked, rising ever so slowly.

"Indeed," I responded and got up as well. It was time to plug in.

I love playing music, and I especially love playing music at Boy's Weekend with these boys who I have known so long and share so much history, musical and otherwise. Even though we meet once a year, our first notes sound like a continuation of the song we started 12 months before. These boys, who are successful, well-groomed, well-paid professionals by day, are also serious musicians. Without a doubt, there are egos and occasional conflicts, but mostly we are friends who just love to play and are honored to share a basement. Although I have struggled with my own musicianship since my parents bought me a red plastic snare drum in sixth grade, I am, for the most part, comfortable here.

If pressed, I guess I would call myself a rhythm guitarist. For me it's all about the rhythm, my first instrument being drums—in an apartment, no less. When playing with the Boys I like to find a place in the music that isn't too crowded. Sometimes I lock the groove, sometimes I hold the middle, sometimes I dance around the edges. Sometimes I forget the chords. I am happiest when we move past the song's boundaries and start to jam, not knowing where we might be headed, trying to keep moving forward, occasionally taking my turn in the driver's seat.

That day in the basement studio, the music surrounded me just as the "special" pancake was loosening the screws of my consciousness; inner doors were flying open. Moments of uncertainty gave way to complete clarity, and vice versa. Occasionally I remembered where I was, but not once did I think about keeping my sperm cool.

It seemed like a few hours down there, in the music, but time had become elusive. I was surprised that it was still daylight as we emerged from the basement. It was nice to know there was nowhere to go, no worries, no hurries, so I sat on the couch next to three slouched Boys.

"Who is the greatest bass player?" Anthony asked, out of nowhere.

Neal was the first to speak, "I once saw Cecil McBee do a 10-minute solo in a dark bar called Bradleys. Listening to him, I forgot there was any other instrument than the bass."

"I wish I had been there," I said. "I would have to go with Jaco, there was one Weather Report show at the Beacon, where he opened the show with a ten-minute drum solo. That's right, drum solo, and then he picked up the bass. What a concert."

The hours did eventually pass, and my thoughts turned to the cooked onions. It would have been a shame to waste them, and although no one seemed particularly hungry, they most certainly would be looking for food before long. I walked into the kitchen to search for a beverage and some inspiration. Tommy was pouring himself a large orange juice. "So Eddie, let me know when you're ready to start dinner? I want to help."

I looked at the clock, it was almost nine. How did that happen? "How about now?" I suggested.

I walked onto the porch where I had stowed the bags of food and kitchen utensils to assess the situation. Mushrooms, cauliflower, spinach, peppers. A plan was coming into focus. I dug out all six boxes of mushrooms and handed them to Tommy along with a big stainless steel bowl that I'd brought.

"How about you start with these? Wash them in lots of water, give them a good rub to make sure the dirt is off, cut off just the tips of the stems, then we'll quarter them. I'll show you the size when you're ready to start cutting," I said.

"Actually, I'll show you right now," I continued, grabbing the cutting board and plucking out a mushroom. After a quick rinse, I cut off the tip of the stem and chopped the rest into quarters. "OK, this is your sample size. Keep these pieces in the bowl for later reference. It's good to cut everything the same size; that way they will cook evenly."

"Yes boss," my sous chef nodded.

Tommy is an attentive listener who offers everyone a shoulder to lean on. He has a son a little younger than Ellena; the two of them have a great time when they see each other, which is not often enough. As Tommy and I prepped the vegetables, his gentle calming nature got me talking.

"I was thinking about not coming," I told him, "but I'm really glad I did."

Tommy turned to me with a look of concern. "Why is that?" He asked.

I gave him a rundown of the last 10 months: diagnosis, doctors, weird diets, chronic uncertainty.

"I'm so sorry; I didn't know," he responded.

"Well, I don't talk about it much," I said. "It's hard on many levels. Many people I know have one child or no children, so it feels weird to complain about only having one daughter."

"That's crazy—you know you can talk to me, to us, to any of us. Wow, I know several people who are also having trouble. IVF treatments, other procedures. I know it can be really hard. Charlene's sister just went through it."

"Well, we're still trying," I said, "but not this weekend."

Tommy's empathy was real, and reassuring. I realized that I had been avoiding telling anyone my awful secret, but I wasn't sure why. It wasn't intentional. What was I afraid of? That I would sound pathetic, foolish, self-centered? That the Boys would publicly demean my sperm?

There was no shortage of assistant chefs, prep cooks and general kitchen help at BW. As I looked around the kitchen at the remaining ingredients and pondered my course of action, Doug and Neal sauntered in, offering to help.

"Let's see, we have cauliflower and spinach," I pronounced to no one in particular.

They looked at me and shrugged.

"Okay, Doug, how about cauliflower?"

"Sure," he smiled, as I grabbed another cutting board, a knife and a head of cauliflower. It was time for another demo. "First flip it over and cut down partially through the stem; then you pull it apart," I explained as I cut the cauliflower and separated it into two pieces with my hands. "Keep doing this with the smaller pieces. The point is to let the cauliflower break evenly along its natural lines—otherwise you get lots of crumbly pieces." I then demonstrated slicing from the top down as an example of The Wrong Method.

"Neal, let's use the big pot for cleaning the spinach. Give it a good soak, lift the leaves out and drop them into the colander. Lift, not pour," I emphasized, "so the dirt stays in the water." I pointed towards the big pot on the floor. Neil leaned down and lifted it up.

I stood back, surveying the scene and pondered my next move. Initially I had pictured a mélange of veggies sitting atop the steaming pasta, but Doug was cutting the cauliflower pieces quite a bit larger than the examples I'd left him. The spinach and mushrooms were probably better on their own anyway. So why not prepare the cauliflower separately? Garlic, paprika, olive oil, topped with a little Parmesan cheese, then gently browned under the broiler.

I had almost forgotten—it was time to start cooking the pasta! Neal was done cleaning the spinach, which freed up the large pot.

"Hey Neal, it's time to cook. How about filling your spinach-cleaning pot with water and putting it on the stove? About two-thirds full should be enough."

"Yes, sir," Neal responded as he filled the pot, and hoisted it onto the back burner. Fortunately, John's high-end stove had a turbo setting.

When cooking large amounts of pasta, I am always reminded of my last year in college and an end-of-year party that I helped plan and execute. We diverted $1500 from the off-campus college rainy day fund to host our final send-off with two bands, 10 kegs of beer, and a pasta-and-salad dinner for 400. I was in a group of 10 that arrived early to chop garlic, wash lettuce and cook sauce. As none of us had ever cooked for large groups, we had not considered how much time we'd need to cook pasta for hundreds of hungry mouths. After the first batch of spaghetti was strained and we watched the water slip down the drain, we realized our predicament. It would take at least another hour to bring the huge pots of water back to a boil and cook another batch. It was a long night of serving spaghetti—and near the top of my ten-best-parties-ever list.

Then years later, after my restaurant closed, in an attempt to turn despair into total abject suffering, I got a job as a waiter—a banquet waiter, no less—at Tavern on the Green in New York City. This was indeed a strange phase in my culinary career, spurred on by my misguided notion that because it was enjoyable to wait on tables as an owner of my own restaurant, it would be fun to do it for someone else. My short tenure at the Tavern coincided with the running of the NYC Marathon. On the night before the race the Tavern had a tradition of feeding roughly 10,000 runners and guests a rather sad-looking plate of pasta, bread and salad. It was a fairly low-quality, high-carb meal intended to promote brand name items from well-known sponsors: designer bottled water, energy bars and deodorant, to name a few. For the entire week leading up to the event the kitchen staff worked day and night cooking pasta. Huge garbage pails filled with pasta cluttered the kitchen. For many years, I would do my best to encourage potential runners to eat their Marathon Eve meal at home.

Both of these experiences instilled in me a profound appreciation for pre-cooking pasta.

Jeff entered the room and observed the goings-on with a quiet intensity born out of a carefree day of rock 'n roll and medicinal pancakes. "I'm here to help," he announced, opening one of his special selection cabernets and pouring out five glasses. "Here's to the kitchen crew!" he cried, raising his glass.

"The Kitchen Crew!" was the rousing refrain.

We swirled and sniffed and aspirated and sipped our wine as only well-cultured oenophiles could. Kitchen work does tend to attract the more sophisticated palates. For a moment we remained in a circle, quiet, a team of guys working together for the greater good: a beautiful meal. For the second time in as many days I felt tears welling up, because the blanket of this Boys Weekend was providing warmth and comfort, allowing me to relax. Being with the Boys made me realize how alone I had felt fighting this battle.

Truth be told, although we shared long history and knew each other quite well, discussing sensitive subjects was not one of the more popular BW pastimes. Usually we had to sift through layers of work politics, landscaping concerns, bad neighbors and plumbing problems before we'd venture into stuff resembling human feelings. But something about standing there in a circle of the familiar faces of my friends made me speak.

"You know, like I was telling Tommy before, I considered not coming this weekend," I squeaked out, looking around at the eyes locked on me. Taking a sip of wine, trying to slow my breath, I went on. "It's been a rough ten months. Basically, Julia was told that her hormone levels were too high and she wouldn't be able to have another child." Another deep breath, another sip of wine. "Julia's working on all sorts of therapies—diet, exercise, herbs—much of the time, I don't know what she's up to. I felt weird leaving her alone with Ellena when I know she's not in a good place. But she told me I'd be crazy not to go. I think she was right. It would've been a big mistake to miss this," I said, "I'm glad I made it!"

Jeff raised his glass again "I'll drink to that. I'm glad you made it too!"

"To Eddie," added Tommy and everyone else joined in.

Nothing more was said, but I felt like they got it. They got me. I didn't have to hide anything from these guys. There was no judgment here.

Feeling distracted in the aftermath of my confession, I almost forgot that we were in the midst of preparing dinner until out of the corner of my eye I noticed the steam rising from the pot of boiling water. With most of the prep done it was time to start cooking!

"Hey, Neal, can you grab the pasta? It's in a bag on the floor by the window. Four pounds should be enough. Throw it in the pot and just keep stirring for the first minute or so to make sure it doesn't clump together."

I found my large rondeau behind stacks of empty bottles and put it on the stove. "And now the sauce! Any volunteers?" I asked, looking at Jeff with raised eyebrows.

"You sure you want me doin' this?" Jeff replied.

Jeff loves telling the story of his first attempt at cooking flan. We were sharing an apartment on 111th Street and Broadway. I got home late one night after the dinner shift at La Caravelle and noticed a tray of flan on the stove which was still hot, apparently having just been taken out of the oven. It had a very thin consistency and obviously needed to be cooked more. No one was home, so I put it back in the oven for another 15 minutes until it was firmly set. A couple days later I came home to find Jeff standing over a new batch of flan. "I don't understand it," he said. "I made it the exact same way two days ago, and this time it's like yogurt."

"Oh oh, I forgot to tell you that I put that batch back in the oven; it needed more time," I said. We laughed for days.

Jeff was actually one of the cooks at the aforementioned college party. He's no stranger to the kitchen, and though he is a bit tentative when left to his own devices, he is great at following directions.

"We'll do it together; have some faith." I assured him "There's a jar with cooked onions on the bottom shelf of the downstairs fridge. Let's give them a bit of color before we add the mushrooms. In the meantime, we should start on the salad and garlic bread."

Jeff returned with the onions just in time to drop them in the hot pan. It didn't take long for the translucent slivers to start sizzling. The smell was even more intoxicating than the cabernet! I called my coworkers over. "See how they're starting to stick to the bottom, and the pan is starting to brown?" I asked, handing Jeff a glass with about an ounce of water. "Now pour this in, and keep stirring."

"Wow," Tommy and Neal said in unison, looking over our shoulders as the water lifted the brown off the pan and onto the onions.

"More color!" I instructed. "Let's do it one more time, and then add the mushrooms." It was a good feeling to be back in my element, in control, seeing the puzzle pieces slowly transform into a meal. It made me realize how little in control I had been feeling lately. Focusing on a simple concrete task—plus the buzz of the wine—was a much-needed respite from the pressures of the baby chase.

"So how do you know how much to make for so many hungry boys?" Doug asked.

"Well..." I stopped and took in the scene around me: bags of produce, cases of wine and beer, pots and bowls and knives on tables, cutting boards overflowing with mushrooms and spinach and cauliflower. I took another sip of the cabernet and continued. "For me it's been mostly trial and error. There's the analytical voice within me saying: 'A five-ounce portion size times the number of mouths to feed, plus the number of side dishes, divided by the number of hours since the last meal, times a smoothing coefficient of .125.' Then there's an intuitive voice that says: 'This doesn't look like enough, because it's Boys Weekend, and we can't run out—and what if Joe, Stan and Ian show up in time for dinner?' But mostly it comes from just doing it a few hundred times."

Jeff, as always, was the perfect lieutenant. With only minor prompting he added four spoons of garlic to the onions before adding the mushrooms. "Keep stirring so they don't stick," I reminded him. The mushrooms cooked quickly; that super-charged burner was indeed super. "OK, now the spinach," I said. "Stir a little, then cover the pot." I noticed that my glass was empty. "Hey, any more of that special Cab?" I called out. Andy quickly filled my glass. After a minute, I lifted the pot cover and handed Jeff some garlic, diced chilies and tamari to round out the sauce.

"What do you think?" I asked, as he sampled a spoonful.

"I like it," Jeff nodded.

He passed me a spoon. "Hmmmm, that is fucking good," I agreed. My hand shot up in the air, and Jeff reciprocated the high five with a triumphant grin. "Let's add a tad more soy and chilies. Once we add the pasta, it'll lose a little kick—it's gotta be strong enough to cut through the haze of Boys Weekend!"

It was close to midnight—time for dinner. I had been waiting until the last minute to make the scallops—large fresh sea scallops that I sliced in half and marinated in garlic, olive oil, salt, black pepper and rosemary. Two hot sauté pans, one minute on each side was all they needed. I then deglazed the pan with white wine, adding a little cayenne and a little soy sauce. Done!

"OK, it's time to eat!" I announced to the kitchen crew, and word spread quickly.

Twenty-one chairs were squeezed in tightly around two tables. The salad, bread, pasta and scallops had been set out on the counter, and the Boys were already serving themselves. I went back in to the kitchen to get the roasted cauliflower from the oven, and when I returned everyone was looking at me. Tommy started the chant: "Eddie, Eddie, Eddie!" and soon The Boys were all chanting my name and clapping and stomping, and I was clapping too. I felt their appreciation deep down. I bowed and pointed to my sous chefs and said with difficulty, "It was a team effort."

I was almost the last to the table with a plate of food and noticed a fresh glass of an Italian Barola in front of my plate. I stood, raised my glass and waited a few moments for the room to quiet down. "I would like to thank you all for giving me the opportunity to shine. Here's to us and may we forever be boys!"

"Boys!" echoed around the room, fading quickly as we all returned to our meal.

It was quiet when I opened the door to the apartment and deposited my gear at 3 PM. I tiptoed in, careful not to awaken any possible nappers. I heard singing coming from the bedroom and slowly opened the door. Two heads turned my way and two voices squealed: "Daddy's home, daddy's home!"

I met Ellena halfway across the room and hoisted her high above my head, then close to my body. She was laughing as she kept repeating, "Daddy om, Daddy om." I put her down, then grabbed Julia, who was now standing beside me, and lifted her off the ground as well.

"So, how was it?" She asked.

"Good," I said, smiling broadly at my two girls. "It was good."

Roasted Cauliflower

The cutting takes more time than the cooking. My family cannot stop eating it. One head is just barely enough.

1 head **Cauliflower**
1 tsp **Olive Oil**
½ tsp **Garlic**
1 tsp **Salt**
1 tsp **Grated Parmesan** or **Romano Cheese**
¼ tsp **Black Pepper**

Cut Cauliflower into thumb sized pieces always cutting down through the stem and then breaking apart the flowers.

In a bowl toss the Cauliflower in Garlic Oil and add Salt and Pepper.

Place on tray and sprinkle with Grated Cheese.

Broil under high heat until golden.

Leave in hot oven with broiler off for a few minutes if not cooked enough.

Serves 4-6.

Chapter Eleven

A STAND-IN

"Some of us think holding on makes us strong
but sometimes it is letting go."

HERMANN HESSE

The leaves crunched under our feet as we made our way up the well-manicured suburban street. It was a crisp fall day in New Jersey, and we were about to pick out the mother of our child.

Julia and I were looking for 153 Clausen Drive, which turned out to be an off-white split-level house, nearly identical to all the other houses we had just passed. According to our directions, we had to proceed through a little gate and down a path on the left to a side entrance, far removed from the prying eyes of neighborhood gossips. We rang the bell, and as we waited I found myself hoping no one would be home. A second ring, and it seemed like I might get my wish, when finally a woman in her late twenties with a brisk air, stylish bright red eyeglasses and matching lipstick opened the door.

"Welcome," she said, "You must be Julia and Ed, I'm Erica, Charles' assistant."

We shook hands. Her grip was unusually firm; my palms were sweaty. She led us down the hall to a room with a stiff gray couch, two chairs and a mahogany coffee table. "Have a seat. Charles will be with you shortly," Erica offered, then turned and walked away.

Julia sat in one of the armchairs, and I took a spot on the couch, looking around the room for clues. Wood paneling, a lamp with a nautical motif, a gray rug with orange flecks. An ordinary, rather dull living room. Somehow much too ordinary for the extraordinary reason we found ourselves sitting here.

On the coffee table were several colorful binders. At first I stared at the closed covers, uncertain whether to delve any deeper, but after a few minutes curiosity compelled me to open one. After all, why else would they be in this room with us? As I turned the pages, I saw photographs—pictures of young women, mostly sitting in suburban living rooms. "These are the contenders," I half-whispered to Julia.

"Maybe you shouldn't be looking at them," she replied. "We should wait for Charles."

But I couldn't stop looking. I was sucked in. Each two-page photo spread was devoted to a different surrogate. There were a couple of shots of her alone sitting on a couch or smiling in front of a row of kitchen cabinets, another with what must've been her husband and a couple more that included the children. Each of the women had two or three kids. I studied their smiles, wondered what compelled them to do this, imagined them pregnant with my child and started feeling progressively more uncomfortable.

After twenty minutes Charles entered the room. "I am sorry to keep you waiting," he said, extending a hand in Julia's direction, then in mine. Clad in a neatly tailored light grey suit and yellow tie, Charles was a fifty-something man exuding the confidence of a competent deal maker. "Good, I see you've gotten acquainted with some of the candidates," he said, noticing the open book.

"Having been through this myself, I understand the kind of stresses infertility causes, and we want to do all we can to make this a joyful experience."

I surprised myself by being more direct than usual: "Well, so far the experience has not been all that joyful," I said. "It would have been nice to have a little introduction before being left here for twenty minutes with these books."

"I sincerely apologize," Charles responded. "There was some miscommunication between myself and my assistant. Be assured that we take this very seriously and have the highest concern for your well-being and will make every effort on your behalf."

I nodded, satisfied with marking my territory. I felt like I didn't have much to lose. We were simply here to learn what surrogacy was all about, to understand our options.

Charles continued, "How about we look through the books together and I can answer any questions you might have." He had a faint accent that was difficult to place. Boston? Philadelphia? Croatia?

Julia came over to the couch, and I flipped back to the beginning and started turning the pages. Hearing Charles' commentary made the smiling faces of the women more relatable. They had names, families, histories.

"Oh, yes, Karen; she's a lovely lady. Two children of her own and this is her second time with us. She birthed for us two years ago and is ready to do it again."

Some of the women were quite attractive, others less so, but all I could think of as we kept picking up each binder was, how did it come to this? Were we really contemplating planting my seed into the body of one of these women? Were we really ready for me to have a child with a complete stranger? Suddenly I was so flooded with gratitude for my daughter, I started feeling lightheaded, and if not for Julia I would've gotten up right then, mumbled an apology and made a beeline for the exit.

Julia's voice pulled me back into the room, "How exactly does this work?" she asked.

Yeah, I thought to myself, how does this work? Does the woman's husband inject my semen into her with a turkey baster while they kiss passionately and listen to Verdi? Am I in the next room just in case there's a slipup?

"We place ads in newspapers throughout the country, and my wife Connie and I travel to meet the applicants personally," Charles explained. "We have a battery of psychological tests to determine unconscious motivation and screen out women who might have a difficult time after the birth. We reject ninety percent of the applicants. In the last four years not one of the birth mothers in our program has changed her mind. We've arranged eleven births so far."

Eleven didn't seem like a vast statistical sample.

"We feel it's important to know what makes each woman choose to bear a child for someone else," continued Charles. "Surrogacy is a way for some of them to work through their traumas. One young woman was told that a pregnancy could help cure her endometriosis and prevent her own infertility.

"Of course, there are some women who find the money useful: to buy a car, renovate their kitchen, start that college fund. The average fee for our services is twenty-four thousand dollars, out of which ten thousand goes to the surrogate."

We really had no idea what this might cost. I was expecting it to be in the ten to fifteen range. Twenty-four seemed high. But was it too high?

"How are we involved with the woman? Can we interview her? Can we visit her?" I asked.

"Your relationship with the surrogate is totally up to you," explained Charles. "Some people prefer no personal contact. Others have the surrogate live with them for the last month of their pregnancy."

"That must be cozy," I remarked, thinking about our one-bedroom apartment.

Julia seemed pretty eager to head for the door, and I was happy to join her. She gave a quick glance in my direction, then reached into her purse, produced an already prepared $300 check and handed it to Charles.

Although he offered to drive us, we had plenty of time before our train and decided to walk.

"What about adoption?" I suddenly heard myself say and immediately regretted opening the subject which both of us have successfully avoided since the diagnosis.

I expected Julia to close down, but perhaps because of our surreal visit with Charles, she didn't seem to mind hearing what I had to say.

"I really do believe that we are good lovers," I said. "I mean that we know how to love, and children are easy to love no matter where they come from."

"Yes, we most certainly are good at loving. That's one thing I'm really, really sure about," she said, slipping her arm under my elbow. "You know, in the old country I hardly ever saw anyone who didn't look like me," she continued, slowing down her gate as we walked through the quiet suburban street.

"When I first came to America, it was like I landed in some fantasy world with so many people from so many different places, different languages, different looks. I was always telling my aunt and uncle how beautiful Asian and black children were and how I one day wanted to adopt an Asian or black child. They laughed at me, thought I was crazy. Not that it surprised me—my uncle once nearly passed out when my black boyfriend showed up to pick me up.

"So yeah, I think I would be into adopting a kid but I'm not there yet. Maybe I'll get there next month or next year…I can't do it now."

"I get it. I was just thinking it might take the pressure off trying. But, okay. Not like we have time on our hands to start shopping for adoption agencies and filling out reams of paperwork. I can't imagine it's so easy to start that ball rolling."

"I'm scared of something, but it's not the paperwork," she said. "I don't really know what I'm scared of. I just don't want to go there now."

"Got it. Subject closed."

"For now," she replied.

Nearing the train station, we passed a dog walker. He eyed us suspiciously, though his terrier was more interested in a pile of leaves. Did he know, I wondered, that we were there to buy a baby?

Tahini Dressing

Tahini can be used as a dip or a dressing or spread. You can adjust the water content to create the desired consistency. A wire whisk makes the mixing easy.

1 cup **Sesame Tahini Paste**
½ cup **Water**
1 Tbsp **Lemon Juice**
2 tsps **Garlic Oil** (From Minced Garlic Infusion)
¾ tsp **Cumin**
½ tsp **Salt**
½ tsp **Black Pepper**

Put Sesame Tahini Paste into mixing bowl.

Slowly add Water whisking gently at first, so as not to splatter contents.

After the paste thins a bit add Lemon Juice and Garlic Oil.

Add other ingredients and more Water if needed for desired consistency.

Chapter Twelve

SUGAR AND CHAMPAGNE:

SHIFT HAPPENS

"A party without cake is just a meeting."

JULIA CHILD

"Geography was never my best subject," Julia told me. When we took trips, she would reluctantly read the map, but usually she left the navigation to me. Our baby journey was taking us into uncharted territory, and although there was no map, Julia did the navigating. She read the books; she made the phone calls; she uncovered the next new fertility enhancing legume. We had left the main highways with all the official signs belonging to the medical establishment. They were no longer helpful. As Julia lost faith in the healers she gained faith in herself, in her own sense of direction.

Something had changed. The journey appeared to have stalled, but when I asked if this meant we were settling for a family of three, Julia's answer was always a resolute NO. The trips to New Jersey and Chinatown had been replaced with mysterious late-night sessions in the kitchen or our spacious black and white tiled bathroom. These were the only two places where Julia's peculiar ministrations wouldn't disturb Ellena or myself. Was she meditating? Weeping? Talking to herself? Speaking to her ancestors? I wasn't sure. All I heard was an occasional quiet moan.

Julia had become diligent about keeping her journal on the night table where she would furiously jot down notes as soon as she woke up or at times stopping in the middle of a conversation to run off and "write it down before it gets lost." When I asked to be enlightened as to what exactly was going on, all I got was a quick smile and a shrug feigning ignorance.

They say a happy wife makes for a happy life. I didn't know exactly if I would call her current state "happy," but she was much more at peace—as if she no longer needed to prove anything to her doctors or me, or most importantly to herself.

Although several weeks earlier, we had RSVP'd our non-acceptance of Bill's 40th birthday invitation, Julia had a change of heart and lobbied for going. Vivi was free to stay with Ellena. It looked like we were about to have our very first official date since Ellena's birth.

The night of the party was carefully planned out, down to choosing the one bedtime story that never failed to lull Ellena to sleep. Sure enough, her eyelids drooped just as the hungry caterpillar had finished his way through the apples, pears, strawberries and cherry pie. I carried her over to her crib and tiptoed into the bedroom. Those first few minutes were crucial to maintaining her sleep-state.

There was no need to rush; we still had plenty of time to get ready. This definitely had all the requisite features of a real date: a babysitter, a three-hour window, a chance to wear the one remaining cool shirt left over from my clubbing days.

Still, as we sat in the taxi it felt like we were getting away with something. We left Ellena with a sitter on a regular basis, so this shouldn't have felt like a big deal. Except that it did. It was different to be leaving the apartment for something as frivolous as a party. True, if all went well, she'd stay asleep and never know we were gone.

Julia appeared absorbed in her own thoughts. Until, as if on cue, we turned to each other. Julia spoke first, "She's still sleeping, right?"

"Right," I said, putting my arms around my wife and pulling her close. "She's sleeping, and I have a hot date with a hot babe."

Snuggling up, she grazed her lips lightly over my cheek. "You are a very likeable person, Eddie Baum. Do you know that?" she asked, sliding her hand up my thigh. "And you deserve to get everything, everything, everything you want in life. You do."

I do have everything I want, I thought. Don't we both have everything we want? We could want more, but let's not let the wanting more take away what we already have.

The joint was already jumpin' when we showed up. A sea of familiar faces doing the two-step on a crowded dance floor. Bill loves to dance, he made sure the music tickled everyone's funk bone. Minutes earlier Julia might've been unsure about leaving a sleeping child with a sitter, but with P-Funk careening out of the speakers, she didn't need a whole lot of prompting. In her off-white silk blouse tucked into a pair of tight-fitting jeans, she shape-shifted into the Woman-in-White I once saw dancing at a bar in Fair Harbor. Only this time she was my partner. We moved as one, in a spontaneous funk ballet.

Robert was right about good dancers making good lovers.

Except when lovemaking feels like your one last chance at getting your wife "with child," the best of lovers turns into a pathetic loser. But I didn't think about that at that moment. I didn't think about anything at all.

Not until it was time for champagne and cake, and there it was again—the reminder that we were set apart from the carefree cake-eating crowd. Champagne and strawberry shortcake were not for us. Alcohol and sugar were at the top of Julia's no-go list.

To my surprise, Julia gave me a quick smile, raised her glass and took a few deliberate sips. "It's a date, remember?" She reached across the table, pulling me toward the dance floor.

"One more dance, and then we'll go. Okay?" I followed her lead as usual, but not before I emptied my own glass.

"We have to do this more—break all the fucking rules," she said, touching my cheek. Soon we were out in the street hailing a cab. It took only a few seconds for an empty yellow car to stop.

"I like kissing in the back of a taxi," my date whispered, glancing toward the driver. "It's too bad we never did it in the back of a car."

Ellena must've sensed that we were back, because she stirred the minute the door closed behind Vivi.

The date was over, but we were both radiant. We were more than parents; we were dancers and lovers and even partiers.

While Julia rushed to look in on Ellena, I logged in to work to check on the progress of my monthly update. Working late at night always made me hungry. The bowl of rice and vegetables left over from dinner hit the spot. It reminded me of a paella I had many years ago, when I was still a free man: free from the burdens of putting food on the table, and keeping my sperm cool enough for procreation, free to hit the road at a moment's notice.

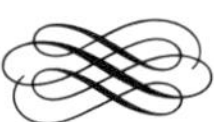

"Bonjour, Jean."

"Bonjour, Georges."

"Je voudrais te presenter Paul Martin…"

I repeated this dialogue in sixth, seventh, eighth and ninth grade French class, and never got much further. After six years of being force-fed a foreign language, I still wouldn't have passed my final New York State Regents Exam without Mathew Bloom, who generously and discreetly allowed me to copy his answers. When I did finally get to France, my experience playing charades proved more useful than all my years of Junior High and High School French.

On my first visit to Europe I was amazed to meet people my age who were proficient English speakers, having gained their stellar skills in a classroom. It was possible to learn another language after all!

My dismal performance in Ms. Kelly's French class kept me from attempting to master another language until I started working in a French restaurant. Although the menu, chef and waiters were all French, the language I craved to learn was Spanish. In the New York City restaurant scene, Spanish is the language of the kitchen. Busboys, dishwashers and porters are almost all from South and Central America. They usually get paid in cash and speak little English. It was a necessity to learn their language just to keep the kitchen running. I started with a few nouns, *cebolla, pescado*, and adjectives *caliente, rapido,* then moved to some verbs *trabajar, dormer.* I was hooked. My fellow workers were delighted to teach me new words and extremely patient with my halting progress. Unlike the Parisians, they didn't seem to mind my Brooklyn accent.

I hatched a plan to move to Spain and find a cooking job. My goal was to really learn Spanish, and what better place to learn than at the source, the nation of bullfights and conquistadors? My CIA training would be an asset and would smooth my transition. I would finally live out the dream of cooking my way around the world!

It was a cold winter day when I arrived in Madrid, Spain, with a Gortex raincoat, a Spanish-English dictionary and high hopes. I found a cheap *pensione*, then two weeks later found a cheaper one, and three weeks after that a nicer and still cheaper one. I did a lot of walking around the city, spending hours in book, music and department stores, avoiding conversation but attempting to soak up as much language and culture as possible. I studiously read my Spanish Grammar Basics: Level One. The Prado, the national museum, became my favorite resting spot, especially between 2 and 4 in the afternoon, since that's when everyone cleared out to concentrate on their two-hour lunches.

Slowly, I became less and less unnerved each time I had to speak Spanish and eventually became confident enough to procure a Michelin Guide and go knocking on kitchen doors asking for work. It quickly became apparent that this was not the typical way of job hunting in Madrid. My inquiry was usually met with an expression of surprise, followed by a stream of largely incomprehensible verbiage. They say in language acquisition, repetition is the key. Maybe that's why the phrase, *lo siento, no tenemos una posición disponible* ("I'm sorry, we don't have a position available") was the first sentence I learned to say with ease. Although it was a rejection, it was always spoken with courtesy and compassion by the chefs I encountered.

After three days of visiting Madrid's finest restaurants, I was questioning my resolve and reconsidering my plan, wondering what the restaurant scene was like in Barcelona. On the fourth day my fortune turned, and the chef at El Circo sent me to their corporate offices, where I was greeted by an NYU graduate, a trim young man named

Placido who bubbled with enthusiasm. In addition to the upscale El Circo, his family owned a chain of American-style cafeterias; they just so happened to be looking for a "Culinary Institute alum" to help these restaurants become more American. Wow! "Here I am!" I exclaimed.

Both their search and mine had ended. I proceeded to spend the next six months working in several of the Madrid restaurants owned by the company, drafting the first official kitchen manual.

Most of my own suggestions, like French toast and cooking the tomato sauce longer than 30 minutes, were dismissed as too ambitious. This was, after all, a successful business that was not interested in rocking the boat. All they wanted were a few minor enhancements. Adding an Avocado Burger to their menu was as "authentic American" as they were willing to go.

As the only American Chef in town, I became quite a hit at parties during the year I spent living in Spain. My culinary skills were the calling card that allowed me to gain access to the usually exclusively women's domain, *la cocina* (the kitchen), a warm room full of copper pans, hanging plants, Moroccan tiles and worn family photos. A woman named Carlita once showed me a heavy iron pot that had been in her family seven generations. Men rarely entered this female sanctuary. Whether it was the fault of too many years of domestic segregation or the Spanish señoras intimidation factor, I soon realized that I was seeing a secret world unknown to my entire gender.

Most Spaniards were unfamiliar with other cuisines. Stir-fried veggies and chopped liver left them speechless. The three main ingredients I encountered were olive oil, garlic and salt. In some homes, they were the only ingredients. The herbs or spices common in the kitchen closets back home such as oregano, thyme, rosemary, cumin, or sage were nowhere to be seen.

Initially I was opposed to the idea of using olive oil for cooking. It has a strong flavor and will burn at a relatively low temperature. Now, however, I've gotten used to it. The taste has become so familiar to me that it never intrudes. For stir fries, salads, and even pancakes it's a healthy choice as long as you don't overheat it. Oil of any kind should not be left on the heat to the point of smoking.

Paella was one of the few Spanish dishes I had prepared before my arrival in Madrid: a rice stew served with an assortment of meats, seafood and vegetables, usually cooked all together. In Spain it is served in many restaurants as an appetizer and, unlike in the U.S., is usually one of the least expensive items on the menu. *Paella* is a good way to clean out the refrigerator, as scraps and leftovers are easily stirred into the dish. The fact that "*Paella Colorante*"—an intoxicating blend of corn starch, salt and FD &C Yellow No. 5—is sold in Spanish stores as a replacement for the real key ingredient, saffron, shows how popular the dish is. The name derives from the pot typically used in its preparation, which resembles a Chinese wok. It was not until I was visiting my friend Enrique's family in the town of Casillas, an hour outside Madrid, that I got to taste an authentic *paella*.

Before we got there our host had filled the *paellera* with rice, chicken, cod, carrots, onions, garlic and saffron, then placed it, covered, on a bed of hot coals in a large stone fireplace in an outdoor patio. After we arrived, I soon found myself helping out in the kitchen while discussing sponge cake recipes and the New York City nightclub scene with the ladies. After several hours of wine and conversation, we sat down to eat. Our hostess was profusely apologetic for having forgotten about the *paella*, leaving us with a somewhat overdone version of the classic Valenciana dish. But to our collective surprise the slightly smoky stew seasoned with saffron and rosemary, which was growing on the hillside next to their house, was delicious. A simple meal in a simple, welcoming home.

Although we might try, it's impossible to separate the food on our plate from the faces of people around the table, the laughter, the stories we hear while eating. That *paella* was the sum of all those things—and no doubt my memory has elevated the experience over time. Which might be the reason *paella* has never tasted quite the same.

When I owned my own restaurant, customers would sometimes stumble upon it by chance and be ecstatic about their meal. Quite often the same person would return, and wind up being disappointed. It has taken me a while to realize it wasn't the fault of our cooking. The dissatisfied repeat customers were usually hungry for more than the fish of the day; they wanted to relive their surprising initial experience. Because of the lack of expectations on their first visit, you could say that they "over-enjoyed" themselves, thus raising their expectations for their subsequent visit much too high to ever be satisfied. The second entrée was almost invariably a letdown; their expectations prevented them from fully enjoying the food on their plate. Usually I never saw them again. However, the few that made it back a third time got to appreciate the meal for what it was. They often became regulars.

How much of my desire for another child was about my expectations of having a family of four? Was this obsession with the way I imagined things should be, robbing me from cherishing the treasure of our threesome?

Forbidden Rice Risotto

Although they are both Rice dishes, it might be a stretch to call Risotto the Italian version of Paella. Aside from the common ingredient, both dishes have different regional variations and are well known around the world. Risotto is creamier. Forbidden rice adds a nutty flavor and silky texture to this variation.

2 med **Onions** - ¼" dice (3 cups)
2 **Celery** stalks - ⅛" dice (¾ cup)
2 tsps **Garlic** minced
1 Tbsp **Olive Oil**
1 tsp **Salt**
6 oz **Mushrooms** (White, Crimini, Bella) thinly sliced (3 cups)
2 oz **Shitake mushrooms** - Thinly sliced (1 cup)
1 ½ cups **Forbidden Rice**
3 Cups **Water**
1 **Yellow** or **Orange Pepper** - ⅛" dice (for garnish)
1 Tbsp **Parsley** - chopped (for garnish)
1 tsp Parmesan Cheese grated (optional)

Rinse Forbidden Rice 3 times and then soak in water for several hours if possible (the more it's soaked the quicker it will cook and the more easily it will be digestible.)

In a large pan (that has a cover,) brown Onions (see page 179.)

Add Celery and Garlic, keep stirring.

Cook for 2 minutes and then add Mushrooms, keep stirring and cook another 3 - 5 minutes.

Add Rice and Water.

Add Salt and Pepper, stir well.

Bring to a boil and then simmer, covered, until Rice is tender, about 30 – 45 minutes, depending on how long it soaked.

Check occasionally if there's enough liquid. It should be creamy. If it gets too dry add some more Water.

Top with extra small diced Peppers (Yellow or Orange look good), chopped Parsley and a sprinkle of grated Parmesan Cheese.

Serves 6-8.

Chapter Thirteen

PRODUCTION

"I don't know the question, but sex is definitely the answer."

WOODY ALLEN

Sex was not something I ever imagined becoming a chore.

Julia and I were married one year and three weeks after we met. The ceremony took place at a friend's loft in the upscale neighborhood of Gramercy Park in downtown Manhattan. I did the catering, which involved buying bagels, smoked salmon, egg salad, whitefish salad and salmon spread from Zabars, and contracting out a few side dishes. My soon-to-be sister-in-law Susan volunteered to make Hungarian crepes with poppy seed filling, and my CIA classmate and master pastry chef Nancy made a velvety smooth flourless chocolate cake which was the true hit of the party.

That night we stayed at the Essex House on Central Park South. In addition to the sweeping view of Central Park and the luxurious cream-colored bathrobes, the "Honeymoon Package" included a bottle of not-totally-terrible champagne and a 10% discount. We ordered a turkey club, french fries and assorted sorbets from room service. Then we ate in bed, both of us wearing our fancy bathrobes.

My wedding night. Not exactly something I had fantasized about since boyhood. Still this was not a night like any other. What would wearing matching rings do to our chemistry? I wondered. Would the consummation of our vows be tempestuous like the lovemaking of Rhett Butler and Scarlett O'Hara in Gone with the Wind? Would our legal bond lead us to new levels of passion?

After we finished the sandwich and a bit of the champagne I looked at Julia. "What now?" I asked.

It seemed like a perfect time to get on with the consummation, but I had not quite factored in the aftershocks that followed the seismic shift of exchanging vows. My hopes for all-night husband-and-wife unbridled lovemaking gave way to a good-enough 30 minutes, which was actually far better than I should have expected considering how stressful the day had been. After all, it's not like we hadn't done it before. Turned out our intimacy was just the right intensity, enough of a release to calm us and ready us for the first good night's sleep in days. It felt good to be married, though it would take time to get accustomed to the white-gold ring on my finger.

About three months later we were dining at Kashmir, the Indian restaurant down the block, when Julia mentioned how nice it would be to get out of town for a few days.

"How about the Catskills?" I asked.

"I wonder if the Nevele Hotel is still open?" she asked.

"Wow, the Nevele! You know the Nevele?"

"Of course! Everyone knows the Nevele," she replied. "I worked down the road from there during my second summer in America. We used to hang out in the coffee shop. It was the only place open after 9 PM."

I hadn't thought about the Nevele Hotel in years. When I was a kid we used to spend a few weeks each summer at my grandparents' house near Ellenville, New York. Down the road were the Fallsview and Nevele Hotels. The Nevele was quite a bit more upscale; visits there were saved for special occasions. Usually I would only gaze at the lush grounds and ten-story high tower as we passed by on the way to the Fallsview for a milkshake or a game of miniature golf.

"Did you know Nevele is 'eleven' backwards, because 11 brothers built it?" I asked.

She didn't know. We booked three nights.

The hotel had not changed much in the 27 years since I had been there last. It was as if the clocks had stopped at 2:30 PM on January 12, 1963—the pinball arcade, the 100-foot ski hill complete with towline, the linoleum rec room where we watched youngsters lip-sync to Billy Joel and Madonna at the teen talent show, the threadbare carpet in the huge dining hall beneath tables piled with plates of mediocre roast beef and chicken parmesan. It was a pleasant break from the City, but not quite enjoyable enough to stay for the entire three days of our reservation. We decided to cut our trip short and cancelled the last night.

During the next three months, we would irreverently refer to the Nevele weekend as our honeymoon—that is, until we boarded the plane bound for Los Angeles.

A trip to California sounded ideal, a place I knew from a few visits and wanted to share with Julia: Yosemite, soaring redwoods, secret beaches, blood-red sunsets over the Pacific.

For the first few days we stayed with a friend in Santa Monica, three blocks from the beach and three worlds away from the Upper West Side of Manhattan. Our host, David, a recent émigré from Manhattan and a doctor at LA County Hospital, worked three 12-hour shifts a week in the emergency room. This practically gave us our own apartment.

We were preparing to get an early start on the second day and walk over to Venice Beach. As we sat on the couch, a sea breeze drifted in, convincing us to postpone our expedition. It felt so nice to have nowhere to go, to waste a morning. We napped a little and snuggled. Gradually the snuggling became a bit more inspired, and suddenly our clothes were on the floor.

"Let's not use it," I said, pointing to Julia's diaphragm.

"Are you sure?" she asked.

We'd come close to "doing it for real" a few weeks before, but had gotten cold feet. We needed more time to sit with the notion of having a child. I guess two weeks was enough, because now it felt right.

"Pretty sure," I said with a big smile. It was clear Julia didn't need much persuading. So why not now? I thought. Could there be a better time?

It was like getting our marriage contract finally signed by the judge. It was official! Perhaps it was tearing down the contraceptive barriers that had been separating us; perhaps it was being witness to the unfolding of our shared future; perhaps it was finally having sex for its intended purpose. Whatever the reason, what ensued was the deepest, most dramatic and intimate physical love I'd ever experienced.

There are three types of good sex (and a thousand types of lousy sex—but that's a different story). After the first type, you think, "My lover and I just had great sex!" After the second type, you feel one with all creatures who have ever merged in physical intercourse: mollusks, octopi, frogs, spiders, crocodiles, woolly mammoths, horses—all sexual beings everywhere. After the third type, you don't remember where you are or who you are. You feel like you've allowed yourself to be swept up by a mammoth wave and have abandoned all control over where you might land. We had that third type of sex in Santa Monica.

We could see palm trees from the couch and feel a light wind from the ocean as we held each other and drifted into a sweet sleep. Eventually we took that walk, a long, relaxed stroll down a white beach as the sun set over the Pacific. Finally, we reached the Green Tree Café in Venice Beach and had a pair of mocha lattes. So this is what all the fuss about honeymoons was about, I thought.

We arrived back in NYC the same day as Julia's period. Our child was not yet ready to show up. Julia returned to teaching social studies and Russian to middle-schoolers. I dove back into my computer studies, but we were a different couple, having ventured a bit further down the road toward our family.

Sitting at the small round table in what was formerly Julia's one room studio, now our common home, I was engrossed in my programming assignment when I heard keys in the door. It was already 12:30. My homework for that night's class would have to wait. Julia was a blur as she entered the room, dropping her bag, unbuttoning her shirt and slipping off her skirt in one fluid motion as she slid into bed. She hadn't called in advance today, so I was a bit delayed in reaching an equally primed and ready state. We only had 15 minutes. Julia had to be back at school by 1:00 P.M. Although we'd heard it was better to give sperm a few days to recharge [*See Sperm Boosting Suggestions in Julia's Afterward], we had decided to use "the more the merrier" approach and make love as often as possible, including Period 4 lunch. I was finding this protocol quite enjoyable and was prepared to collaborate 100%.

The following month, Julia's period was late. It had been six weeks since our return from California and six weeks since her last period. She stopped by a lab on her way to school, and at 4:00 the nurse called with the news. "Yes, you are, Ms. Indichova, you're pregnant. Congratulations." We held each other, elated by the thought of becoming parents. It was that easy. Wham, bam, here I am. Seven and a half months later I was holding Ellena Indich Baum in my arms as Julia was wheeled out of the operating room under general anesthesia from an emergency C-section.

When it came time to start trying again, we had no reason to expect anything to be different. This time, I was the one coming home for lunch—43 minutes for travel, 1 minute to neatly fold and hang my suit, shirt and tie, 4 minutes to shower and dress — which left 11 minutes for getting down to business and on particular efficient days, lunch. Plus, all this had to coincide with Ellena's nap! Still, it was definitely worth the trip. By the end of the second month, due to an ever-increasing pile of work, I found it harder to get away. We switched strategies, deciding that once a day was sufficient, in fact better, according to the sperm-hoarding theorists.

After the diagnosis, sex was not quite so carefree. It was fraught with expectation, and seemed more like an industrial process. It was far from a wave lifting, can't-get-enough romp, and as each month slipped by, so did a little more of the passion, as if living with a young child wasn't enough of a deterrant. Were we doing it less? Not really, but it felt that way. It became yet another chore to check off the list, along with buying diapers and arranging playdates.

Nonetheless, we perpetually strived to improve our technique. We heard that the missionary position was best, and Julia raising her hips after intercourse would give the sperm a gravitational assist. Morning sperm was said to be healthier, so we set the alarm for 6:00 AM.

Then Julia informed me that saliva inhibited sperm motility—another reminder to stay on track. Foreplay had shrunk to shorter and shorter intervals. It was unnecessary, in fact detrimental. After all, this was serious business.

Things got even more serious the day Julia got a call from the doctor. As a principal investigator of her experiments, she was having her hormone levels tested each month to observe potential fluctuations. With her FSH dropping to 21, the fertility specialist was calling to let us know that with the lower hormone levels, IVF with injectables became an option. But we must hurry because these numbers might not last. This news caught us off guard. Julia was at first hesitant, but then resolutely refused the idea of treatment.

"Something is working. I'm not messing with it," she insisted, not even looking at me.

"How could it hurt to try the drugs just once?" I pleaded. "What if this really is our last best chance? You're not a doctor. What makes you think you know better than this woman who has probably done it for years."

There was no getting through to her. We were staying the course. But because her numbers were so low, my wife thought we should ramp up production during ovulation week. Lunchtime was not so workable, but we managed an early morning intercourse shift, then again in the evening.

As we moved through the week, our expectations rose. Each encounter had more gravitas; each pelvic thrust had a bit more riding on it.

I was at work when Julia called. "I'm so sorry," she said. "I got my period."

"It's okay," I said. "We'll keep trying. I've got to go. Bye"

I hung up the phone and could feel the blood rush to my head. It was not okay. I felt like Sisyphus, rolling a stone up a mountain only to have it roll back each time. Did we indeed just squander our last best chance? I grabbed my coat and headed out of the building. I walked across the street to Grand Central Station and stood on the balcony overlooking the main terminal room. I thought about the times my friends and I would come here as teenagers. We'd get high after school, stroll up Park Avenue, stop in Benson's, a high-end stereo store, spend an hour listening to Pink Floyd and the Moody Blues in the boutique sound room, then head up to Grand Central for rush hour. We would stand on this very spot looking down mockingly at the sea of commuters scurrying towards their suburban homes and lawns and slippers. "That will never be us," we'd tell each other.

It did make me smile and put things in perspective. Just a bit.

I timed my arrival home just before Julia left for her evening class. I couldn't face her. Then I made a point of going to bed before she returned. I feigned sleep as she came to bed; she didn't touch me. This was hard, way too hard. It was her fault. We should have done the drugs. I was spinning this around in my head until the long day caught up with me, and I drifted off to sleep.

I was up early and left the house before anyone else was awake. On my way to work I passed through Grand Central and glanced up at the balcony. The irony did not escape me.

It was an ordinary non-stop data day at the office, and it was 6:00 PM before I turned around. My voice mail was blinking. I had missed a message.

"We are looking for a guitar player for our singing group. You could come and try out for us," I heard Julia say, speaking in a formal tone, then heard both of them break into giggles. My heart ached.

I grabbed my coat and rushed to the subway. I needed to get home. Julia met me at the door. She was intent on not letting me stay at arm's length.

"I am so sorry," she said. "I just couldn't do the drugs. It wasn't the right time."

She hugged me, and I felt cracks in my shell. I hugged back.

It was late at night when she crawled into bed after feeding Ellena. I reached over and stroked her hair; she drew me close. She was sleepy and so was I. We held each other as our hands and arms and hips met in the darkness.

"Shouldn't we be saving it for production? It's almost that time," I said.

"Fuck production," Julia whispered.

Here it was again, the wave. It was different than the one I remembered. But for once I had the good sense to let go of expectations and not care where I'd land.

Spicy Garlic String Beans

Timing is important here. Making sure the string beans are cooked just enough but not too much before sautéing. That the pan is hot and the garlic doesn't burn. And when the soy sauce is added that there is enough, but not too much liquid. They should be dry when done. It's worth the effort. If it's not spicy or garlicy enough feel free to adjust the quantities of cayenne and garlic. Just remember to go slowly, you can always add more, but you can't take away.

1 lb. **String Beans**
1 tsp **Garlic** - minced
1 Tbsp **Olive Oil**
1 tsp **Soy Sauce/Tamari**
2 Tbsps **Water**
pinch **Cayenne**

Cook the String Beans in a large pot of boiling Water.

Remove when still crunchy and place in cold water, to stop the cooking.

Heat Garlic and Oil in large pan.

Just as the Garlic starts to turn brown, quickly add the String Beans and stir well.

After the Beans are coated with Oil and Garlic, add Soy Sauce, 1 Tablespoon of Water and Cayenne, to desired spiciness.

Keep stirring until dry. If they need to cook longer add another tablespoon of Water and keep cooking and stirring until dry. Be careful to not let them burn.

Serves 4-6.

Chapter Fourteen

ANOTHER CALL

"Only those who risk going too far can find out how far one can go."

T.S. ELLIOT

It was a regular day at the office. The phone rang two short rings, signifying an outside call. In the approved manner specified in Section 4.2 of the Bear Stearns Employee Handbook, I answered, "Bear Stearns."

"I'm pregnant," she said. "I just had a test. We can't get too excited; it's very early. The doctor is giving me progesterone. It's supposed to regulate my levels. He said I should go home and not go to work."

"Yes, go home," is all I managed to squeak out before my vocal chords stopped cooperating.

I was expecting this. I had always been expecting this, because I never lost hope. Still, I was stunned. I hung up the phone and quickly stood up—where was I going? I wanted to tell someone, but it was too soon. There's an unspoken rule that you share your joys at the office but not your disappointments. This was a joy that could quickly turn into a deep disappointment.

I could not sit still. It was too early to go home. I needed some air. I grabbed my coat and headed outside. Grand Central was calling me again. It was close and larger than life, with enough history and volume of humanity to absorb my tentative jubilation. It's a place you can scream without being heard. I was terrified that this was a mistake. That somehow the lab screwed up and gave us somebody else's test results. After all, they said Julia couldn't get pregnant, and now she was. Were the doctors just wrong, or was this a miracle? I felt like Abraham, the biblical patriarch who was 100 years old when he learned his wife was with child.

The view from the balcony overlooking the main terminal with the spectacle of tiny people threading through the vast room has always been grounding for me. Except this time, I didn't want grounding—I wanted to run and dance and leap and cry a joyful cry. It was almost 3:00. I thought I should go home, because I was useless to Bear Stearns at that moment. I headed back to work to inform those who needed to be informed and walked smack into the crisis of the day: the database was spitting out ones instead of zeroes and rejecting all efforts to save the day's closing prices. The CMO trading desk was complaining that their P & L was off and someone was screaming, "This is the third time this month we can't close our book!"

Going home was no longer an option. It was a bona fide system meltdown, and my adrenaline was gushing, just like in my cooking days. When I worked at La Caravelle, one of my first restaurant jobs, some days I would not prepare quite enough puréed spinach for the night's service, which would lead to me running the length of the kitchen into the walk-in refrigerator, grabbing the cooked spinach, running across the room to the industrial-size Hobart mixing machine, hooking up the strainer attachment, forcing through the spinach, running back to the stove, grabbing a large sauté pan on the way, removing the iron middle ring of the flat top stove to expose the serious heat, adding the spinach and half a quart of cream to the pan, and stirring like a potion-making witch-on-crack, while the chef took a break from yelling at the new broiler cook to instruct me—at the top of his lungs—to give the FUCKING SPINACH to the waiter. *Merde alors*!

I was feeling some of that same rush. My "database" adrenaline was now mixing it up with my "Honey, I'm pregnant" adrenaline. I should have been lifting out of my seat and shooting through the ceiling, but I'm a well-trained professional, so I managed to sit in my chair long enough to fix the problem and be on the subway by 4:00 with the promise that I would log on to my computer the minute I got home.

I did my Olympic-style speed walking from the subway, up Broadway and across 100th Street, past our doorman—before he had a chance to turn his head—and into the stairway. I only slowed down at the ninth floor; the last three flights always seemed a little steeper. I stopped a moment to catch my breath before entering our apartment. Julia was in bed but not asleep. She was now porcelain and must not be jostled. She looked at me with 80% joy and 20% terror. I was feeling more like 60-40.

"I'm OK," she said. "I just have to be careful. He told me to take it easy. It feels good to lie down."

Seven months and eighteen days later, Adira Indich Baum became the fourth member of the Indichova-Baum family.

Pasta with Onions and Avocado

Best to use ripe but not overripe avocados. Don't let it cook too much and don't over-stir. The avocado adds a great silky texture.

¾ lb cooked **Pasta** (Your choice)
2 med-large **Onions** - sliced (3 cups)
2 tsps **Garlic** - minced
1 Tbsp **Olive Oil**
2 Tbsps **Water**
1 Ripe **Avocado** - ½" dice
1 tsp chopped **Parsley**
Salt and **Pepper** to taste

In a large pot brown the Onions (see page 201.)

Add Garlic and cook 2 minutes. Add Oil and Water and cooked Pasta, season with Salt and Pepper, stir well.

Scoop Avocado out of shell with a spoon and then cut into cubes.

Add Avocado to Pasta, stirring gently to avoid mashing it all.

Garnish with Chopped Parsley.

Serves 6-8.

Chapter Fifteen

SISTERS

"Children must be taught how to think, not what to think."

MARGARET MEAD

On a visit to the kitchen I notice some red liquid dripping from the counter onto the floor. The source of the scarlet puddle is a mason jar overflowing with cabbage and carrots. It is covered with a dish towel. Fermentation is in progress, and it is indeed working. Looks like Ellena forgot to put the plate underneath to catch any runaway brine, again.

She has recently returned from interning at a homesteading project in Missouri, where she helped with construction, scything, harvesting sorghum, cooking over an outdoor wood stove and playing mandolin in a gospel band.

Ellena is drawn to the earth and seems most content living in a community setting, planting, watching things grow. On early morning walks she points out nettles, red clover and mugwort growing wild in our backyard. And last night she walked in with a bucket full of sap from two sugar maples out front.

Her face lights up when she talks about the people she's met on her adventures—the sun-haired, ocean-eyed magical six-year-old girl, who made her laugh and draw and sing and ride broomsticks, the young man who was breeding his own squash and carving the most perfect spoons, a couple raising earthworms, which, Ellena explains, are highly effective natural agents for soil improvement.

"Our soil could use a few dozen bins of those worms," she tells me.

I'm not quite ready to start farming worms, but I admire the depth of my daughter's passion for causing as little harm as possible to the earth that feeds us.

Her sister Adira is less interested in farming, but derives pleasure from the food that results from it, and the tastiest preparation of that food for human consumption.

She walks down the produce aisle ignoring the dark green heads of broccoli, the beaming orange peppers and the vibrant reds and yellows of the rainbow chard. She's looking for tomatoes, juicy and ripe. After the third pass, she presses "Home" on her speed dial.

"Yeah?"

"I can't find any ripe tomatoes. These are green and hard—really hard! I need them for the sauce."

"What about canned tomatoes?"

"No, I want fresh."

"How about cherry tomatoes?"

"Let me check hold on… There's only one container."

"Mix them with the canned."

"Ugh! You're so stupid," she replies and hits "Call End." She hesitates for just a moment, then grabs the cherry tomatoes and two cans of organic diced plum tomatoes. She can make this work. There's still some fresh basil in the garden and some oregano too.

Minutes later she's home, spilling out her newly-acquired vegetables onto the counter. She grabs the cutting board and rifles through the knife drawer for a sharp tool. Looking through the onions, she finds two that are just the right size, small-to-medium, and cuts the ends off first. Wait, where are the goggles? Onion-cutting requires nerves of steel and swimming goggles. She tightens the straps to prevent her eyes from filling with tears.

Cut the ends off first, core-side up, then slice in half down the middle. Now peel the skin (her least favorite part). Fingers curved, gripping the half onion, sliced-side down. (They are curved to prevent bloodshed.)

Adi leans the blade against her knuckles as a guide. She can do this with her eyes closed but decides to keep them open. It doesn't take long for the onions to become a neat pile of small uniform pieces, which she hurriedly scrapes off the board and into the pot while adding some olive oil. She knows this is radical; heating olive oil is frowned upon in the Indichova-Baum kitchen. Something about toxic Oxygenated Aldehydes. Undaunted, she proceeds, gaining momentum.

She's comfortable taking control of a situation, even a bit too controlling at times. When motivated she displays an incredible force of will. Nothing is beyond her reach, whenever she chooses to reach. In her 17 years she has spent many hours in the kitchen in the company of a professional, Culinary Institute of America-trained chef. Her knife skills and stove technique have been acquired, but her love of food and cooking is her own. She's been reading cookbooks and foodie memoirs for years and looks forward to each new season of Top Chef.

The onions are starting to sizzle. Stirring is essential, especially in the early stages to prevent sticking as they start to sweat. The flame should be lowered now.

Adi opens both cans of tomatoes and gives the onions another pass with the spoon; they're almost ready. The cherry tomatoes are not fun. They are small and roll around the cutting board. It's hard to curve her fingers and keep hold. Her dad walks in. "Use the serrated knife," he suggests, trying not to sound bossy. She hates that it's not really a suggestion but knows he's usually right. "And leave the fresh tomatoes till the end; they'll stand out more," he says, leaving the kitchen. She was about to cook them together.

According to plan, the onions are beginning to brown. Now it's time for the tomatoes. She dumps in one can and hesitates, remembering the golden rule, the one repeatedly cited by the chef-in-residence: "You can always add more, but you can't take away." She has trouble with this one. She likes to add a lot. She is not a fan of restraint. (It's a family trait.)

Her arrival seventeen years ago may have been in doubt, but she rarely manifests this trait herself. She gets her brown eyes and insight from her mother, her love of reading and love of excess from her grandfather, her stubbornness from her dad, her intensity from all of the above. But Adira is more than a collection of influences.

She adds half of the second can of tomatoes, stirs, then dumps the rest in—the cherry tomatoes, too. Looks like there will be leftovers.

She chops the basil and oregano and fortunately finds some fresh minced garlic from the night before. The sauce starts to bubble, so she covers the pot, lowering the heat. She fills the other large pot with water for the pasta. The salad is easy—lettuce, cucumbers, orange and yellow peppers; wash, spin, slice.

She lifts the lid on the sauce. It's hot—a little too hot—and she curses the stainless steel, licking her scorched fingers. She considers her dad's remedy: holding a new burn over the heat, as hot as you can stand it. It's supposed to be like cauterizing a wound and will both prevent blistering and eventually stop the pain, albeit after inflicting quite a bit of immediate suffering. Adira's never quite embraced this method. She prefers cold water.

The sauce is not what she envisioned. Her dad is again peering over her shoulder. "There's some chopped parsley from last night in a bowl on the top shelf in the fridge that you may want to avail yourself of," he offers. "It could be a good addition."

He retreats again to his office. The water is now in a rolling boil, so it's time to add the pasta. She makes sure to stir well after dumping in the bag of quinoa rotelle. Those first few seconds are critical to keep the spirals from sticking and requiring lots of work to separate.

With the pasta cooking, she again stirs the sauce and tastes a spoonful. The flavors are starting to peek out from behind the tomatoes' acidity. If only she had some fresh Heirlooms! Something is missing. She adds a bit more salt but not too much, because her goal is to finish with grated cheese. Maybe that parsley isn't such a bad idea...

Soy Sauce is a staple in the kitchen. Her dad seems to put it in everything. She likes it too, but she's been avoiding it lately, searching for new spicings. Adi is drawn to innovation, but she's also wary of it. She dislikes failure. She hasn't yet learned that no one develops a skill without failing. (Maybe this was never explained to her?)

She almost forgot the fresh whole wheat baguette, which was amazingly still in the bread bin at the store at 5 PM. She heats chopped garlic with equal parts olive oil and butter in a small pan—not too much, just enough to serve as a medium for the garlic. She's careful not to let the liquid brown, heating it sufficiently to release the flavor. Then she brushes the mixture onto the sliced baguette, topping it with grated cheese and placing the bread in the hot broiler.

The pasta is almost cooked, not soft but not too chewy, either. She'll give it another two minutes. She tastes the sauce again, then adds a handful of the parsley. She tastes again, sprinkles in a little more salt, some fresh black pepper and the rest of the parsley. This is actually starting to look and taste like tomato sauce.

It's been three minutes—time for the pasta. She must hurry! Where's the colander? Like her father, she prefers towels to potholders—not that she could find a potholder, anyway. The towel should be dry; she's made that mistake before. Using a wet towel with a hot pot can lead to burnt fingers and spaghetti all over the floor. She drains the pasta and dumps it into a glass bowl—then peeks in the broiler. The garlic bread is ready. It's a glowing honey-brown.

The garlic bread is a special treat intended for her sister who should be arriving any minute for a weekend break from college roommates.

The timer goes off, and, as if on cue, Ellena walks through the door. She's not one to do much squealing, but glancing at the table set for a feast, she inhales the aroma of garlic and spices and smiles.

Minutes later, the four of them are sitting together again. Dad reaches across the table with one hand holding each of his daughter's hands. Mom sits between the two girls as always, offering an improvised benediction. The great chef Jacques Pepin says the most important ingredient in a recipe is love. Clearly, that essential item is present in this meal.

"It's not so good," Adi apologizes, carrying the sauce to the table. "I really wanted fresh tomatoes."

But it is good—really good—and as the two girls eat their first forkful, they look at each and, for reasons only they understand, they laugh.

Fresh Tomato Sauce

This is a great summer dish, I like it lightly cooked and slightly tangy.

1 med **Onion** - ¼" dice (2 cups)
1 stalk **Celery** - ⅛" dice (½ cup)
1 ½ tsps **Garlic**
8 med **Tomatoes** - ½" dice (4 cups)
pinch **Cayenne Pepper** (to taste)
1 tsp **Soy Sauce/Tamari**

In a large pan sweat Onions (see page 201.)

Add Celery and ½ the Garlic and cook till dry (almost sticking.)

Add Tomatoes, cook until a bit of the acidity is gone, about 20 - 40 minutes.

Season with Cayenne, Soy, Salt and Pepper.

Serves 6-8.

KEEP WALKING DAD, I'LL MEET YOU HALFWAY

AFTERWORD BY JULIA INDICHOVA

"...to be right and useful, one must accept a continuing divergence between approved belief—what I have elsewhere called conventional wisdom—and the reality."

JOHN KENNETH GALBRAITH
THE ECONOMICS OF INNOCENT FRAUD

I can't possibly start this afterword without acknowledging how profoundly grateful I am for this book's author, the two beautiful human beings we have been able to raise together and the life we continue to be blessed to share.

Over the years, Ed and I have often talked about what it was like for him when we first received the diagnosis, what would we have done had we not conceived? How have our lives and our marriage been altered by this unplanned voyage? I'm thrilled that those conversations have now morphed into a memoir I get to offer my clients as an additional source of solace and guidance.

In close to two decades of supporting people in birthing their families, I have been particularly moved by the many men who have attended the Fertile Heart workshops and teleconferences. In pretty much every case, when the dad-to-be has shared his reason for attending one of the sessions, he'd say, "I'm here to support my wife. I want to do whatever makes her happy." Most of them play down their own frustration and the depth of their disappointments.

Whether it's the common perception that for a man being vulnerable is a sign of weakness, or the myth of seeing impaired reproduction as a signal of diminishing virility, or any of the myriad possible reasons, I find that men tend to distance themselves from the painful responses evoked by an "infertility" diagnosis.

Even when the trouble is traced to the male partner, it's the woman who becomes immersed in the search for solutions. And since for the most part it's the woman who is prodded and poked, bearing the brunt of treatments, the aspiring Dad is often left feeling powerless.

Yet, if there is one thing that a fertility challenge calls us to affirm, it's that we are far from powerless. Sperm morphology and motility and count are all fluid and changeable, because the multilayered human organism is fluid and changeable. The same way ovarian function and female hormone balance is affected by every thought and feeling that courses through us, so is sperm quality a reflection of our relationship with ourselves and each other, the food on our plate, our history and every facet of our lives.

Having said that, I better add that although we humans are powerful co-creators of our circumstances, there is nothing like baby making to show us that we are co-creators only, not gods. The idea is not to blame ourselves for the obstacles we face but simply do all we can to conceive as conception friendly a space as possible. To do all we can do to meet our children halfway.

In a loving partnership, we are called to be each other's midwives. To adore the person we have chosen to be the mother or father of our child exactly as they are at this very moment. Then, as compassionate midwives we are also meant to co-create a non-threatening, conception friendly space in our relationship. A space in which each of us gets to birth the most fulfilled joyful version of ourselves.

In the early years of Fertile Heart, it was mainly women who signed up for our events. Thankfully that has changed, and we get to welcome more and more couples. I'm honored to include here four stories told by the Dads-to-Be. Some of the couples conceived with the help of medical technology, some through spontaneous conception, and one is a poignant account of an adoption journey. What each of the couples had in common was a determination to follow through and the commitment to keep moving in the direction of their common desire.

Raising our level of wholeness is not a guarantee that the child will arrive on our timetable in precisely the way we wish. But no matter when or how we finally become parents, we want to receive our children into a home where our capacity for compassion and our appreciation of each other has grown exponentially through this extraordinary shared pilgrimage.

- *Julia*

SPERM BOOSTING SUGGESTIONS

If common sense is not convincing enough, it seems every day a new study validates a holistic, health enhancing approach to increasing male fertility. It's an approach that can even save the dad-to-be from heart disease or cancer later in life, since the same imbalances that trigger degenerative diseases are the culprits of abnormal sperm morphology and other symptoms of impaired reproductive function.

Here are a few common-sense and not-so-common-sense ways to keep those life-giving strivers in peak shape:

Don't save it up:
While some literature suggests abstaining from sex prior to ovulation, more recent research shows that frequent ejaculation results in lower DNA fragmentation and better overall sperm quality. Sperm stay alive inside the cervix for 48 hours. So for best results have as much fun as you can during the fertile time of the woman's cycle. Remember that if we're hoping for lively follicles and feisty sperm, we need to turn "production" times into pleasure soaked discovery days rather than chores linked with repeated failures. The idea is to use everything: frustration, sadness and hope, and channel it all into erotic, risk taking, love making. (More on this topic in my *Kiss Me Quick, I Feel Fertile* Ebook.)

Exercise in Moderation:
Whether it's running, biking or fast walking, remember that excessive exercise tends to lower testosterone levels needed for sperm production. Bikers are advised to use a seat with a wide back, instead of a narrow, hard one in order to place more weight on the sit bones rather than on the testicles.

Limit exposure to radiation:
If you're getting an X-ray of any part of your body, be sure to request a lead shield to protect your testicles.

Limit exposure to electromagnetic fields:
An increasing volume of research points toward to an adverse effect on sperm quality with exposure to electromagnetic fields, such as heavy mobile phone use. A landline

might be a worthwhile investment for protecting the dad's and mom's overall health. Aspiring dads should also avoid carrying their mobile phones in their front pockets. Maybe even turn off your cell phone when not absolutely necessary.

Keep cool:
Heating the testicles even a few degrees can sabotage sperm quality. Avoid hot baths, hot tubs, tight bicycle shorts or tight underwear in general. Research shows that resting a lap top directly on your lap can raise temperatures in the scrotum by as much as 5 degrees Fahrenheit in an hour.

Avoid the common sperm saboteurs:
Cigarettes, alcohol, marijuana or opioid painkillers do not make for feisty sperm. Smoking and drinking lower testosterone levels needed for sperm development.

SPERM FRIENDLY EATING HABITS

"No" Foods:

Caffeine – is a highly addictive substance and in the long run it doesn't do much good for female or male fertility. All caffeinated drinks elevate the stress hormone cortisol, which, as noted earlier, decreases testosterone levels and consequently impairs sperm quality. Excess cortisol also accelerates aging, interferes with sleep and causes essential nutrients needed for healthy conception, such as zinc and calcium, to leach out of the body. We know that for women, caffeine consumption has been linked to increased miscarriages, premature births and stillbirths. it is not unreasonable to hypothesize that caffeinated beverages consumed by men may also be harmful.

Junk food – A joint Harvard and University of Murcia, Spain, study analyzed the sperm of young men between 18 and 22 and found that although the men were in good health and had no other issues that might affect their fertility, the sperm of the men who indulged in junk food, especially in transfats, were less likely to fertilize the egg.

Non-fermented soy products – can interfere with the absorption of iodine. Iodine deficiency leads to slowed metabolism, weight gain, fatigue, intolerance of cold and other symptoms of hypothyroidism, an underactive thyroid. Impaired thyroid function has been linked with low count, motility, lower testosterone and an imbalance of luteinizing hormone (LH) and follicle stimulating hormone (FSH).

Herbs to avoid – Echinacea, Gingkgo Biloba and St John's Wort. If the aspiring dad has been using these herbs as immune boosters (Echinacea), or circulation support (Gingkgo Biloba) or as natural antidepressants, it's best to take a break from each of them. Studies indicate a potential link to sperm damage.

Sperm-Friendly Foods:

Low glycemic fruits – Seminal fluid that supports developing sperm contains high levels of antioxidants, protecting them from oxidative damage. Oxidative damage is the main threat to the developing germ cells, a factor that can be effectively reversed with high quality, absorbable forms of antioxidants. Green apples, berries, cherries, grapefruits and grapes are some examples of fruits rich in flavonoids, a nutrient famous for its antioxidant and anti-inflammatory effect.

Veggies:

Green leafy vegetables – are great sources of folate (known in supplement form as folic acid), an essential nutrient for healthy cell division, calcium, iron, beta carotene. The darker the color, the richer the nutrient content. One thing to remember is that kale and chard contain goitrogens, compounds that interfere with the production of thyroid hormones. Cooking helps deactivate the goitrogenic effect. If you suspect hypothyroidism, consider blanching them before you add them to your morning juice of smoothie.

Sea vegetables – *Hijiki*, *arame* and *kombu* are great sources of iodine, calcium and minerals that support thyroid health and overall endocrine function. Consuming sea vegetables is especially important if you're eating fermented soy products.

Fermented Foods – "Live," naturally fermented foods can supply the badly needed allies for raising your intestinal immune system, improving digestion and making sure your internal cleansing organs are in tip-top shape.

Avocado – Source of healthy plant based fats and vitamin E, helpful for repairing damage caused by free radicals.

Nuts – walnuts, pumpkin seeds, sunflower seeds and cashews are excellent sources of essential fatty acids, vitamin E, zinc, L-arginine, selenium, iron and other necessary sperm building nutrients. Nuts can be difficult to digest, which is why you'd be wise to soak them first. Soaking and sprouting nuts neutralizes the potentially irritating phytates and activates the enzyme needed for greater nutrient absorption.

Fish – sardines, wild salmon and herring are excellent sources of omega 3 fatty acids and vitamin E. (Check fish advisories in your area.)

More superfoods and sperm enhancing herbs:

Royal Jelly – a fertility tonic for both sexes, a rich source of amino acids, vitamin A, B-complex including folic acid, iron, calcium, all of which are essential libido boosting and hormone balancing nutrients.

Maca – a popular hormone balancing, libido and fertility boosting superfood, rich in amino acids, fatty acids, calcium and other nutrients. It is usually available in powder form. Since it has a pleasant mild nutty flavor, it can be added to smoothies, cookies, energy bars, pancakes or other culinary creations.

Goji Berries – celebrated superfood with a high level of antioxidants that have been traditionally used in Chinese medicine as male and female fertility tonics.

Ginseng – a nourishing and stimulating herb which supports the endocrine system by strengthening the hypothalamus-pituitary-adrenal axis.

Saw Palmetto – a popular herbal tonic for the entire male reproductive system.

SPERM BOOSTING SUPPLEMENTS

In an ideal world of nutrient rich soil and a diet of wild plants, daily herbal infusions, and organically grown foods, supplements would be obsolete. The truth is that on a physical level, there is nothing that can match the reparative power of whole, fresh, nutrient-filled food.

Eliminating a few of the chief culprits I listed earlier, which tax our digestion and burden our liver and other organs of elimination, can also be a giant step toward a more energized body. (See "Ally in the Cupboard" chapter in The Fertile Female, and "Cleaning the Refrigerator" in Inconceivable, and food related E-books on Fertile Heart for a more in depth look at this subject.)

Having said that, when it comes to overall health and fertility related difficulties, pretty much everyone—whether it's a holistic practitioner or mainstream physician—agrees that supplements can help prevent degenerative disease and increase the chances of getting pregnant and carrying a full-term pregnancy.

To be most effective, the elements in a particular supplement work synergistically. Taking a high quality multi-vitamin developed by a qualified scientist can provide a baseline of nutrients without the guesswork of how much of each compound would offer the maximum benefit.

Below is a list of endocrine-supporting nutrients for the dad-to-be. The best way to start is to check whether or not your multi-vitamin contains these compounds and then consult with an appropriate healthcare practitioner about any additional supplementation based on your symptoms.

Folic acid – Not only is folic acid an essential nutrient for the mom to be, research indicates a link between folic acid deficiency and low sperm count with increased sperm DNA damage.

L-arginine – Is one of the key amino acids needed to insure a robust count, motility and overall sperm prowess. Inversely, low L-arginine levels are associated with low count and motility

L-Carnitine – another key amino-acid is one of the key amino acids for male reproductive health. Similarly to L-arginine, low L-carnitine levels are associated with low count and motility. Supplementation is most effective when combined with CoQ10 and alpha lipoic acid.

Selenium – is needed for sperm production. Low levels of selenium have been linked with low sperm counts.

Zinc – a key nutrient for maintaining optimal testosterone levels and the prevention of DNA fragmentation. A deficiency is linked with low count and motility.

Pycnogenol – is the trade mark name for a pine bark extract rich in flavonoids. Like many plant compounds it is a powerful antioxidant. In a small study, Pycnogenol was linked to increased morphology, which to me is one more validation of the fertility boosting effect of antioxidants.

FERTILE HEART

STORIES OF HOPE

"Hope is definitely not the same thing as optimism. It is not the conviction that something will turn out well, but the certainty that something makes sense, regardless of how it turns out."

VÁCLAV HAVEL

DISTURBING THE PEACE (1986), THE POLITICS OF HOPE

JOSH 37 AND GRACE 40

baby boy conceived through ICSI

Grace and I met at a Jewish dance called the Latka Ball. It was about as cheesy an event as it sounds. We went on nine dates and after the ninth date I called Grace and said, "I am really enjoying hanging out with you, but I don't think this feels like the kind of thing that leads to marriage, so I think we should stop seeing each other."

I'll never live that one down. It's only one of the many times I've been wrong in our relationship. About a month and a half later, we reconnected at a party and started seeing each other again, and we've now been married for three and a half years.

I'm almost three years younger than Grace. So, there is no question that for me, the beginning of our fertility journey really started with the decision to get married. It was one of the first life crises that I had, one of the first places where the way I was approaching the world really hit a wall.

I got reasonably far in my life, planning and controlling and scripting things out. I was going to go to a good school, and I was going to follow a plan. I had a lot of privilege and good fortune, and the decision to get married brought up a tremendous amount of fear.

If my goal was to try to have a perfect life, and I was trying to control everything, how could I look at somebody and know for sure that this decision would be right, 20, 30, 40, 50 years down the road? And really it wasn't just about Grace. It was about, if we get married, what happens if one of us gets sick? Here I was having to make this lifelong commitment, embracing uncertainty, and I totally hit a wall. I was having a lot of trouble, and one of the factors was the ability to have a family.

Grace was wonderful in many, many dimensions, but one of the concerns I had was that she was older than me. In my imaginary world, I was going to marry someone younger, and that would give us a different timeline for planning a family. In the end, I got introduced to a great therapist. Ten thousand dollars' worth of therapy later, I was able to see that happiness is wanting what you have, not having what you want. It sounds like a cliché, but I was really able to re-envision my goals in life. It became more about how I approached the journey and about being loving and joyful wherever the adventure takes us. It's not that I'm able to embrace that every day, but aspirationally that was the attitude I wanted to live by. This all happened for me as the kick off in the decision to get engaged. It continues to be a life long journey, trying to actually live those values.

Just before we got engaged we decided on egg freezing with the idea that this would be a kind of security blanket for us. That didn't go so well. The doctors were not super happy with how Grace responded to stimulation. That was our first signal that this was going to be a challenge for us. That scared me, but I was already seeing my therapist, and had been going through my renaissance, so I received this news with a very different attitude.

We went through the egg freezing process and got 5 freezable eggs. A month and half later we got engaged. In the summer right before we were married, we tried freezing eggs again, but were not very successful.

We had an amazing wedding in September, and we started trying for a baby right away, initially trying naturally for about six months. Because of the egg freezing process, we were already in communication with a number of fertility doctors and getting lots of advice. So even though we were trying naturally, because we had already had these signals, it wasn't like we were shocked when we didn't get pregnant. For better or worse we went in with reduced expectations. And then we escalated through the process. We did some IUI's and two IVF's.

It was already this huge central focus of our life, going thru all these steps. We also tested my sperm about ten times. I had, generally speaking, good count and okay motility, but each time they were not happy with the morphology, and nobody could tell us exactly what that meant. But in the end, that didn't change a ton of decisions for us, because we were going to do ICSI anyway.

We started using a clinic in Colorado and had our five frozen eggs shipped there. We were surprised when only one of them thawed well and fertilized. Usually our fertilization and growth rates were better than that. We'll never know if it was the shipping or something else, but it didn't go well.

All in all, we did two egg retrievals and two IVF cycles and at least 3 IUI's over the course of the first year and a half of our marriage. All unsuccessfully. Except we did get one genetically viable embryo out of the first egg retrieval.

It was a year and a half of science really not working for us, encountering all the frustrations including the cost, and the very challenging dynamics of wondering if anything would work.

Around this same time, Grace stumbled across Julia's website and loved the empowering messages. She got her books and CDs and started working with them, and she wanted to go to the workshop.

I wanted to continue the Western path, and Grace just really wanted to take a break from treatments. It was the first real source of conflict in our marriage. I would say the root of my defensiveness about complementary medicine was my mom's long history of rejecting Western science and seeking alternative treatments that hadn't really worked well for her. So, I have a lot of sensitivity around that. I was completely supportive of whatever Grace wanted to do, as long as we were doing IVF cycles or planning the next treatment. I definitely had some resistance about going to the workshop and working with anyone who was going to tell her that Western science shouldn't be part of the solution.

I blamed Julia for Grace's decision to take a break from treatment. But after attending Julia's workshop I realized that wasn't fair, because that wasn't what I heard. What I heard was a much more holistic message which said that Western medicine can be part of the solution but shouldn't be the only part of your journey. That ultimately was what I always believed, but maybe I believed more in the idea of it than in actually living it. But the further we got and the more we lived it, the more powerful it became for us.

After the workshop, Grace wrote to Julia and joined her ongoing teleconferences. I don't think she missed a single session. They became a real anchor for her.

We went back to Western medicine. We did a triple IVF process and got a total of ten eggs, they fertilized, but in the end no genetically viable embryos came out of that process. That was sort of our last hope. We were really disappointed and frustrated.

At some point we also had a consultation with Marc Goldstein at Cornell after we heard him speak at one of the Fertile Heart Guest Teacher Teleconferences. Mainly we wanted his opinion about whether or not to go through a low grade varicosele surgery. We appreciated that he did not push for surgery at all. He didn't feel it was necessary, and we decided not to do it.

All along both of us continued to become healthier in every way. Julia was an amazing guide for Grace. We still had the one genetically viable embryo from the very first egg retrieval, and we decided to attend the workshop one more time before the transfer.

I definitely came to the first workshop with some resistance, and I mainly came as a support to Grace for whom this was important. The Fertile Heart practice and teachings and the teacher had been a central part of her life for months. By the time we attended the workshop the second time, our journey felt more like a joined process. It's true that we each had different experiences, but it felt much more like something we were doing together and planning together. I remember coming to the second workshop with a little less fear. I knew a little more what I was getting into. It was less to support Grace and more to experience this together and work together before we moved on to the next part of the journey.

We also asked Julia if she would meet with us for a private session after the workshop, and that was also powerful for me. I think Grace had perceived there to be a tension between Julia, as her teacher, and me, as her husband. But during that session we all connected and enjoyed each other and had a great conversation. It felt like a very healing experience.

Our little viable embryo is now a baby boy growing in Grace's belly. We're 26 weeks into a wonderful pregnancy. We are incredibly excited about this baby. What's amazing to me is how little I think about what comes next. We don't know if or how we might be able to have a second child, and I mention it only because I could imagine the old version of me not enjoying any moment of this experience because I would already be worried about what comes next.

As anyone who struggles with fertility knows, it was a challenge for our marriage; it really brought to light the differences in our approach to life. And yet, if you were to ask either of us, we would say, amidst all of that going on, we had a wonderful three years. They were full of blessings, great times, trips, family, wonderful nieces and nephews and incredible friends. I think we would say that we both really grew as people focusing on who we are and not just on our achievements. For Grace, and through her, also for me, Fertile Heart and working with Julia was central to that journey.

DEVIN 43 AND SARAH 43

baby girl conceived spontaneously

I remember the day when Sarah and I met. We actually first connected online. I had been living here in New York just a few months; she had lived here for thirteen years. We went to the same college, UC Berkeley, at the same time. But we met and fell in love here in New York.

We had also worked in the same industry, and, of course, we were both from Northern California. Not that we would have run into each other there, but we had the same home base, same home area. All of that really helped.

Towards the end of that year, it was pretty clear to both of us that this was it, that we'd found the love of our lives and we wanted to be together. One of the benefits of being in your late 30's and looking for somebody is that you really know what you want at that point. We had a conversation about wanting children pretty early on. That was actually one of the questions on the online form for chemistry.com. I had resigned myself to being an older dad, but you don't want to waste your time dating someone if you already know up front that they don't want to have kids. It was something that we discussed right away.

We ended up getting married about a year and a half after we met, and it took about two years before we started trying to conceive. We knew we wanted children, but we also wanted to have some time together. When the time came, Sarah looked at things like IVF and different fertility treatments, because we were past 40. Every website, every book, was telling us how difficult it was going to be. But she is both very natural in her approach to eating and medicine and health overall, and she also just doesn't react well to medication of any kind. For her, to consider treatment would be only as an absolute last resort.

She read Julia's books before we even started trying. We were going to attend the workshop together but I ended up being out of town, so she went without me. The workshop was quite cathartic for her, and she came back excited about finding something she could feel good about doing. She joined Julia's support teleconferences and became very active in that community. She also occasionally worked with Julia privately. She was quite excited about what she was learning.

I was resigned to being an older dad, but I was also sensitive to it because my dad was also older. He was 44 when I was born, and he was not super active. The difference between me and him was that my dad had been in World War II, and he had been injured and actually lost some of his lungs, so he was physically weakened. He was perfectly mobile—you wouldn't look at him and think there was anything wrong—but he wasn't someone who could go out and run around and throw a ball. He was pretty sedentary. I had this association growing up, of having an older father who wasn't physically involved. I had this fear of playing a similar role with my child.

As time went by and we were not getting pregnant, I felt more and more disappointed. I knew that Sarah was also disappointed, but I felt uncomfortable showing it because I didn't want her to feel like I was disappointed with her. It was very difficult for both of us. I didn't know what to say or not say, and sometimes that made it worse.

It was tough for me but I think it was much harder for her. She was internalizing a lot of it. I wanted to pull her out of it, I wanted her to feel better, but I just couldn't figure out what to do or say.

There's no question that in terms of getting pregnant, Sarah did all of the heavy lifting. Having made the decision not to take any drugs, not to do IVF, she radically modified her diet and took all sorts of vitamins and supplements. I was cavalier about the whole thing. I had this attitude of, "you do what you have to do. I'm fine."

After a few months, Sarah asked me to go to the doctor and have my sperm checked. I went into it, very manly, just thinking I'm fine. Why should there be any problem? But there was. My sperm count was fine, but motility and morphology were very low. That was a real shock to the system for me to realize that I was letting Sarah go through this, doing all this by herself. I couldn't do that anymore. I shouldn't have been doing it to begin with.

I started also radically changing the way I was eating. Sarah had been working with Julia's books and on the teleconferences, receiving guidance with those adjustments. I dramatically reduced the amount of sugar I was eating. I also discovered that I was gluten intolerant. My mother has Celiac disease. I stopped eating gluten completely. I also started taking the supplements that Julia recommended.

Sarah kept me very much in the loop about the Fertile Heart work. She shared the imagery with me. Sometimes we did the imagery together. She shared some of the passages from Julia's books with me.

And it worked. I went back to be tested, and three months after making those changes the motility and morphology had improved.

Finally, we ended up going to the workshop together. Since I missed it the first time, I felt that I wanted to leave no stone unturned. What I liked about the workshop was that Julia was not promising miracles, she was not saying that her work would immediately fix everything. She offered a space that helped us open our hearts to having a baby in whatever way it was going to happen. And she offered real tangible tools and ideas that helped me let go of trying to control the whole thing.

As it turned out we conceived naturally a few weeks after the workshop. It was Sarah's first pregnancy at 43. Lena is two and a half, and we are having so much fun with her, we couldn't be happier.

MARK 31 AND DONNA 30

spontaneous conception after 3 miscarriages and high FSH

We were sitting in the office of a Reproductive Endocrinologist to discuss the results of a handful of tests run a month earlier. Hope was in short supply to begin with, and after his diagnosis of a 1-5% chance of a viable full term pregnancy, he offered us a box of tissues and a catalog of egg donors. All hope sublimated, and in its place came devastation, then depression, then despair.

We lost our third pregnancy after 9 weeks.

Feverishly we tried to find someone who could help. We made phone calls and consulted with the so-called experts, scoured the Internet, adopted a dog. Nothing was lifting our spirits.

Then one of the doctors recommended Julia's book, and we found out that she was teaching a workshop. Skeptically, we got in the car and headed to Woodstock. I have never felt such a lack of confidence or hope as I did in those first few minutes of the workshop. If I was skeptical when we left home, I was a real non-believer when we got there. Everything was totally non-traditional—but entirely by design.

We nervously walked into Julia's studio, and the workshop started soon after. I distinctly remember how uncomfortable the room was. All that I could feel was a giant invisible wall. I could see through mine, but not through other people's walls. Nobody wanted to make eye contact. Everyone seemed sad and ashamed. I have never felt such a lack of confidence in a group like I did in those first few minutes.

Then Julia went to work, methodically leading the group through a series of exercises, all the while reading the room and tailoring her approach to our specific collection of cases. Sporadically she zeroed in gently coaxing someone closer to the truth. As stories like ours came out into the slowly opening circle, she kept adapting more exercises to the needs of the group.

This went on for what seemed like a few minutes. I looked at the clock—two hours had passed, and it was time for a break.

At some point that afternoon while being led through a visualization, my life changed and has not been the same since. As I let go and closed my eyes, Julia's instructions summoned vivid images of our future. There, in our backyard my daughter stood above me as I lay on the grass. I pointed at something in the distance. She smiled back at me, and her toddler hair wisped in the wind. I opened my eyes and she was gone. I closed my eyes again, but I couldn't get her back.

I just wanted her back, but she was gone.

"It seemed so real," I said to Donna on the way home. But for her, the images weren't as real or convincing. At first, they felt forced, and she was frustrated. But Donna was determined, and a month or two later, the imagery became completely effortless. Donna joined Julia's teleconferences, and although initially she would not speak up, after a few weeks she began to feel more comfortable on the calls and more comfortable with herself in general.

My hope was renewed by a single vision—Donna's took longer. The despair, though not completely gone, had taken a back seat to hope.

By June, there was still no pregnancy. We found another RE that had a type of low-stimulation IVF for women with elevated FSH. We decided that if in August we were still not pregnant, it might be worth a shot.

By July we were both really happy. It was the first time in two years I could actually say that. We felt great; our love was stronger than ever. Apparently, our daughter knew that too. On our Independence Day vacation, Callie Jean was conceived, and Donna carried her all the way to my waiting arms. As I caught her tiny body in the delivery room, I remember hearing our doctor say "It's a girl!" and thinking to myself, "She just came back."

EVA 48 AND FRANCIS 51

baby boy conceived through egg donation

Eva and I met when I was 41 and she was 38. Neither of us had ever been married. At that stage, I was relaxed as a bachelor. I had moved into a house that I was renovating and I was quite happy. Then I met Eva at a party and we clicked.

A month later in August, I was home for my father's annual memorial, and after I came back I said to Eva, "You better come home with me and meet Mum before Christmas." She gets very excited around the holiday. We were moving very quickly.

Our backgrounds are totally different. Eva's parents are Jewish and my parents are Catholic. Her mum was more relaxed around religion, but for her dad, things were pretty black and white. We didn't know how he would respond to me, but we met and got on just fine. I didn't force Eva down the Catholic road, and she didn't force me down the Jewish road. We respected each other's traditions. As far as I'm concerned, if you're blessing for the good, I don't care what religion you are. I could never understand as a youngster why would anyone have a problem with Jewish people? It was totally nuts to me. My family was completely welcoming toward Eva. They were delighted and had no issue whatsoever with Eva's being Jewish.

I had no intention of getting married, let alone having children. When we started talking about marriage, I didn't really want to have children. Eva just wanted me to be open to the possibility. In some ways, she herself had given up on this, but when she met me, her desire for children got rekindled. She thought, this is somebody who I could have a family with. At first I was happy to go along, but as months turned to years, things became very difficult.

Eva would try to find anything that would make her more fit. She was working on her diet, and not just hers but mine in a way that I thought did more harm than good.
We had been trying for five years before she found Fertile Heart. At that point we had already gone through three failed IVF's, 2 rounds of Clomid and two rounds of Tamoxifen. We spent three years working with a company that concentrated on nutritional balance, and we worked with another company that helped track Eva's hormones. She also had acupuncture and reflexology, but in five years she was never pregnant.

When she read Julia's books and got excited about Fertile Heart, she was 44. Initially I was apprehensive about her getting involved with something new, because when she worked with other people in the past, it would just increase her stress. But with Fertile Heart it looked a lot more positive. I saw that it helped with her anxiety, and she got huge support from Julia. Fertile Heart became a place for grounding herself. She called into Julia's teleconferences religiously. She was now working through whatever was going on for her on those calls, and instead of putting the pressure back on me, she was able to get support with the things that were stressing her.

She became much more relaxed around food; after every call, Julia would suggest to her some imagery and body work, and it became a different journey for her and an easier one for me.

We live in the UK, so I'll admit I was, to a certain extent, dragged to the workshop in Woodstock, but I was happy that I went with her. She got a huge amount that day. I know it generated a reaction in her system. I connected with it as well. It was good to see other men there, supporting their wives, and I felt good that I was doing the same.

I remember getting together with one of the couples, and the guy was there physically, but he wasn't prepared to do anything. He was not even prepared to give up alcohol. I didn't feel he was there for his wife. It made me realize how much I was really there for Eva, and she saw it as well. It was good for my ego to see that I might complain, but I was really there for her.

In December of that year, Eva became pregnant naturally at 45, but unfortunately, she miscarried, and that was very difficult on both of us. But the one thing that became even clearer through that experience was that our love was growing deeper, and we were fully committed to each other.

When it came to making a decision about our next step, the overriding factor for me was that if I made her stop before she was ready, she might agree to do it, but ten years later she might be bitter and angry toward me. I made that point clear to her that at the end of the day, she would have to be the one to say when to stop.

Eva also worked with Julia privately and eventually said she was ready for egg donation. We both called into a Fertile Heart teleconference with an American doctor who was the head of an egg donation clinic, and another call with women who used the Fertile Heart program through their egg donation treatment. That was very helpful for both of us.

We had a choice to go to Spain, but in Spain there was no obligation to reveal the identity of the donor. Eva thought that if she was the child, she would like to have the option of knowing who her biological mother was. In the UK, the child is able to connect with the biological mother. Eva wanted to keep all these options open for the child.

We ourselves had no connection with the donor. It was totally anonymous. We worked with an organization that charged us a fee for finding a donor. We filled out a detailed questionnaire, listing any concerns, the nationality we would like, etc. They have a website, and potential donors contact them for many different reasons. Our donor contacted them because a friend of hers had trouble having a baby, and she saw the pain and anguish her friend went through. We got the photograph of the donor as a baby and toddler, not as an adult. We also got their health history, their education and an extensive personal profile, but no identifying details.

I know that Eva did a lot of work around moving to egg donation on Julia's calls. She also flew back to Woodstock for a second workshop just before the transfer, and she came back feeling much more peaceful about the whole thing.

All along it was a nine-year journey, and we have a beautiful son. He's really fantastic. Sometimes we can't quite believe it that after all this time, he's here with us. Now Eva is back on Julia's calls. She tells me, she is ready for number two.

Epilogue

SOME THOUGHTS ON COOKING

"Cooking is the art of adjustment."

JACQUES PEPIN

This book started out sixteen years ago as a "how-to-cook" book with a short intro about our fertility journey. After reviewing a rough draft with an editor, it became clear that our fertility struggle needed to be the focus of the story. I also felt compelled to share it with the many men, and also women, going through this same challenge. Cooking is a fulfilling, grounding and nurturing force in my life and I wanted to have it be an integral part of my story as well.

Although I wouldn't call this a "cookbook" I do hope you will find the techniques and recipes I have presented here useful. Please remember to use them as a guide. I like to think of them as points of reference and not as a definitive statement. I encourage you to rewrite the recipes in your own image, putting as little or as much of yourself as you are willing and able to impart. Not only will the food become more alive, so will the cooking experience.

I am truly the world's best cook, for myself. I know what I like and how to create it. The amounts of garlic and oil, salt and pepper, oregano and rosemary that I use are to my taste. It is true that after years of training and practice I am good at translating my ideas into dinner. However, as with life in general, it's the misses that provide the best opportunity for growth. As a professional chef, I have learned to temper my own vision with an understanding of how others receive it, and after many years of getting feedback I am confident now that when something tastes good to me it will most likely be enjoyed by others.

I remember some of my cooking experiences before I had any professional training. I would often start out with an idea and as the process unfolded I would be as curious as anyone else how it would turn out. Often the dish was quite good and well received, yet it was different from what I had in mind. It could certainly be viewed as a success, but I was frustrated at not being able to realize my vision. I have just three words of advice: practice, practice, practice.

Eventually I found it easier to turn an idea into reality. This is not to say that I still don't make mistakes or have bad ideas. I do, and I always try to glean something positive from the experience. Even if it doesn't become dinner hopefully I have learned what not to do next time.

So even if you want to follow these recipes to the teaspoon, there are still ingredients that you might want to adjust for yourself. Certain ingredients are hard to quantify. For example, the amount of water used in a soup will depend on many things; from how long it cooks to how high the heat. Salt and garlic, two fundamental ingredients, should vary in quantity mainly due to one's own taste, and almost any seasoning will vary in flavor and intensity depending on its quality and freshness. One teaspoon today may not be enough tomorrow, because it won't necessarily be the same thing. Dried herbs and spices don't always taste the same and they don't stay fresh forever. This holds true for many other ingredients.

Let me restate the rule I always try to follow—"You can add more, but you can't take away." Go easy. You can always add more salt or water, or garlic or cayenne, or soy sauce or whatever, but removing them is like trying to turn that can of black paint into light gray; you'll need a lot of white.

Above all, have fun. You too can become your own best cook. No one knows better than you what tastes good.

Many of the recipes in this book contain onions. My mantra for making soups or sauces has always been: Onions, if you think you've added too many, add more.

The hardest part for me is the peeling, slicing and dicing. Swimming goggles are a big help to keep from tearing, especially when cutting more than one. I find the actual cooking relatively easy. A little salt, added at the start, will help draw out the moisture, hastening the process. Use medium heat and just enough oil to coat the onions. Covering the pan will also speed the process along, but you know what they say: "out of sight, out of mind." Be careful and don't forget to occasionally stir.

Sweating Onions, as the name suggests, is the process of getting them to release their moisture, to the point of translucency. In theory, they shouldn't get any color, but for most recipes, it's not a big deal if they turn a little brown. If they start sticking add a little water.

Browning Onions is what happens when they keep cooking. (Most people refer to this as caramelizing but technically it is part Maillard reaction and part caramelization, two distinct chemical processes.) Start by sweating and then continue to cook as they turn brown. Add a little water and stir to transfer the brown from the pan to the onions (it's like magic). Repeat the process if a darker color is desired.

Diced or sliced Onions can be cooked the same way.

Garlic is another common ingredient in my recipes and I find it convenient to have some on hand so as to not have to chop it for every recipe. Typically, I will mince a head of Garlic and keep it in a small covered glass jar submersed in Olive Oil. The flavor of the Garlic will transfer quickly to the Oil and is great to use on its own for seasoning when you don't want pieces of Garlic. Covered and stored in the refrigerator, it can easily last a couple of weeks. Different dishes will call for different percentages of Oil and Garlic. I often add a little during the cooking process and some more right before serving, adding a fresher Garlic flavor to the dish.

An Oil infusion will easily diffuse in the dish, creating a more even distribution of flavor. This is effective when adding Garlic as a finishing touch, especially to individual portions. It's also useful where you don't have a lot of cooking time—Scrambled Eggs, for example.

Umami, literally translated as 'pleasant savory taste', has recently joined salty, sweet, sour and bitter in the scientific lexicon as a distinct taste. It is one of the reasons you will see Soy Sauce or Tamari in so many of my recipes. It is loaded with the stuff.

The kitchen utensil I would recommend over all others is a sharp knife. It is easier and safer to use than a dull knife which often requires more pressure leading to more serious accidents. Consider purchasing an electric knife sharpener (Chef's Choice makes a range of models).

The second thing on my list would be a heavy bottom stainless steel pot. It will more evenly distribute heat, from any source, gas or electric, and lead to less burnt meals.

Below are the cutting sizes most commonly used in my recipes. More important than getting the size right is being consistent. Otherwise the big pieces will still be hard when the smaller ones are over-cooked.

Extra Small Dice (Brunoise) – 1/8" sides (3mm)
Small Dice – 1/4" sides (6mm)
Small-Medium Dice – 3/8" sides (9mm)
Medium Dice – 1/2" sides (1.25cm)
Large Dice – 3/4" sides (2 cm)

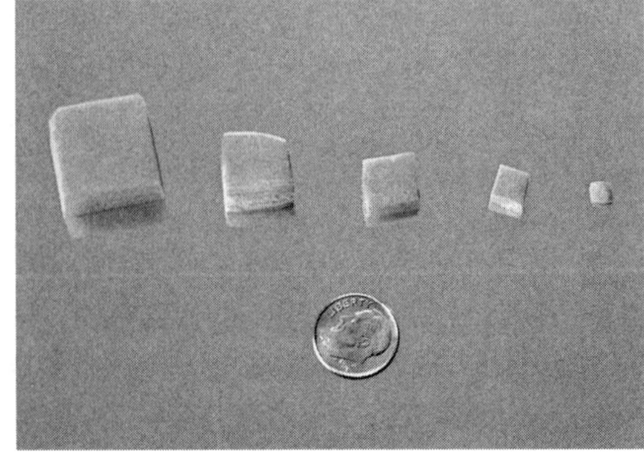

CUTTING AN ONION

Cut both ends off first and then slice in half down the middle.

I find it easier to peel the onion after it's been cut in half.

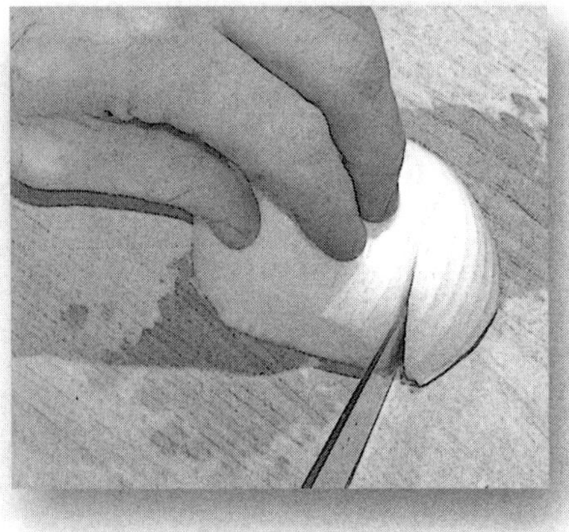

With the cut side down and the core facing away, slice down, but don't cut all the way through, stop at the core. This will hold the pieces together.

[For sliced onions, remove the core and cut all the way through on each slice.]

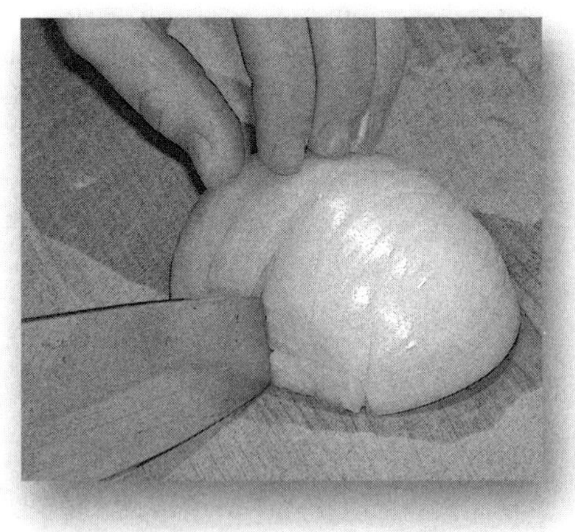

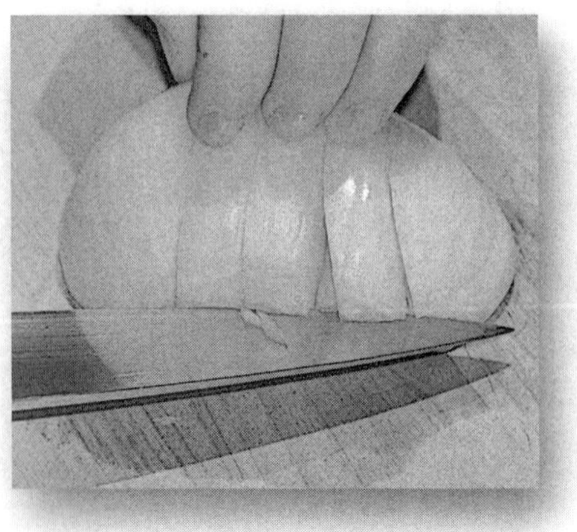

Slice horizontally across the onion, again stopping at the core. Watch those fingers. A sharp knife will make this whole process, particularly this step, so much safer and easier.

Now slice down across the onion, cutting off the desired sized pieces.

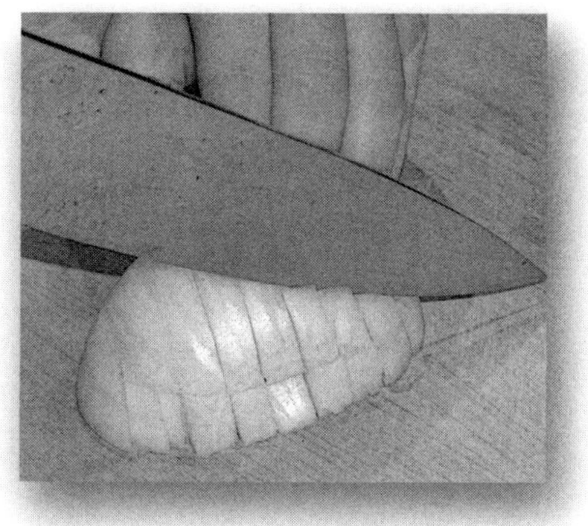

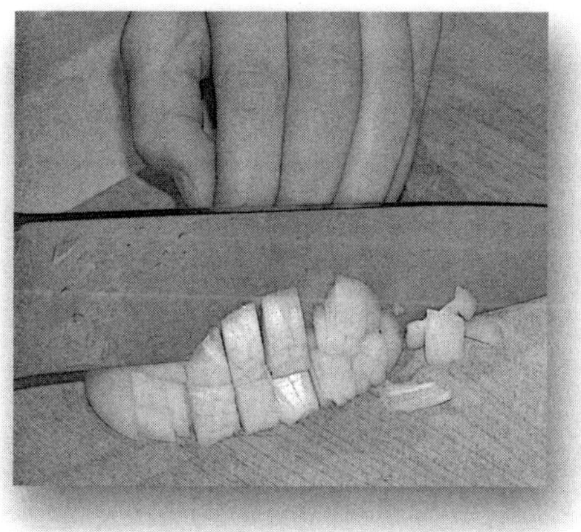

Flip the remaining piece that's too small to hold on its side. Then slice across both ways.

Cut up any remaining big pieces. Keep track of the core. It's OK to put it in a Soup or Sauce that will cook more than a few minutes, otherwise put it in the compost pile, it will be too tough.

Nicely Done.

Recipe Index

10 Roasted Squash Beet Soup

24 Lentil Soup

35 Chia Pudding

49 Kale and Sweet Potato Sauté

56 Herbal Infusion

68 Vegetable Soup

81 Broccoli with Garlic and Cilantro

91 Quinoa and Cold Cucumber Tabouli

100 Veggie Burgers

121 Roasted Caulifower

130 Tahini Dressing

140 Forbidden Rice Risotto

152 Spicy Garlic String Beans

160 Pasta with Onions and Avocado

169 Fresh Tomato Sauce

FERTILE HEART RESOURCES

Books and Ebooks

The Fertile Female: How the Power of Longing for a Child Can Save Your Life and Change the World. Julia Indichova, Adell Press, 2007

Inconceivable: A Woman's Triumph Over Despair and Statistics. Julia Indichova, Broadway Books, 2001

Cooking to Conceive the Inconceivable: One Chef's Journey to Conceive the Inconceivable. Edward Baum, Forward by Marc Goldstein, M.D., F.A.C.S., Adell Press 2017

What to Expect from a Fertility Expert: Tips on Increasing Pregnancy Success Rates from Three Prominent Fertility Specialists - Kindle Ebook. Julia Indichova with Sami David M.D., James Grifo, M.D., Jonathan Scher M.D., Adell Press 2010

The Gift: 3 Friendships, 11 Miscarriages and Ten Thousand Miracles – Kindle Ebook. Julia Indichova, Adell Press, 2017

The Ultimate Fertility Diet: Food as a Fertile Heart OVUM Tool Kindle Ebook. Adell Press 2016

Audio Programs

Fertile Heart Imagery One – An introduction to the Fertile Heart approach to using images to identify the inner physical, emotional and spiritual obstacles to conception.

Fertile Heart Imagery Two – This three-part program builds on the first introductory CD with a more in depth discussion of the Fertile Heart OVUM philosophy. Includes 34 carefully crafted visualizations conceived through more than a decade and a half of counseling.

Fertile Heart Body Truth – Fertile Heart™ Body Truth, one of the key tools of the Fertile Heart OVUM Program, is a fertility and health enhancing movement practice. Through a guided meditation and specific movement sequences Body Truth allows aspiring parents to physicalize and release "issues in their tissues" and transform the body into a reliable instrument of creation.

Egg Donation as an Instrument of Healing – A Two-Part Program with Dr. Frederick Licciardi and Mothers of Children Conceived through Egg Donation, Facilitated by Julia Indichova.

Exploring Holistic Fertility Treatment Options – A panel discussion with four seasoned holistic practitioners.

Video

Meeting Your Child Halfway – A 20 segment video series that opens the opportunity for women and couples around the world to experience the Fertile Heart OVUM Program in the comfort of their homes and with Julia Indichova's direct guidance.

The Fertile Heart OVUM Program – An introduction with an overview of the philosophy and tools.

Fertility Success Stories – Ten-minute video featuring excerpts from the Meeting Your Child Halfway Workshop and Fertile Heart Moms.

The Ultimate Fertility Diet – Beyond Wheatgrass and Green Smoothies – An introduction to food as a Fertile Heart OVUM tool.

Unexplained Infertility – The Good News and the Very Good News – Julia Indichova speaks about the singular opportunity that comes with the unexplained infertility diagnosis.

Fertility Treatments: When They Heal, When They Harm – Lessons learned from spontaneous pregnancies after failed fertility treatments.

IVF: Do It Right or Do It Over and Over – Preparing body and heart for a successful in vitro treatment outcome.

ACKNOWLEDGMENTS

Many people have helped this book along on its scenic path to completion.

Bert and Moira Shaw were among my very first encouragers, guiding me past some of the initial obstacles. I've been blessed to enjoy their company as neighbors, teachers and friends.

The inimitable Martha Frankel inspired and challenged me to keep telling my story. It was an honor to be part of her class of gifted writers. Special thanks to Lynn, Ann, Desiree, Ida, Kathleen and Peter.

My gratitude to Sandy Dorr for wading through the first muddled draft of the manuscript and for offering insights with such kindness and generosity.

Many thanks to Ann Hutton. Just when I thought it was done, she helped me with my very last tweaks that really made it a better book.

Sparrow and I spent many hours in conversation over Hot and Sour Soup and Eggplant in Garlic Sauce. We even spent some of that time discussing the writing of this story. His commitment to this book and wonderful edits were instrumental in its completion. He is a good friend.

Thank You to Joe Pieroni, Tom Grant, Jeff Langer and Nancy Wheaton Langer for taking the time to read an unpolished product and help make it shiny.

Thank you to Bruce Mattel, Dr. Paul Turek and Belinda Anderson for their support and encouragement.

Thank you to the talented Susanna Ronner for her elegant vision. I feel fortunate to be able to collaborate with her.

Dr. Marc Goldstein was among Fertile Heart's early supporters. I am grateful for his generosity and his wonderful forward.

David Andrews has been on our side in a way that few others have. I am privileged to call him my friend and mentor.

Rabbi Jonathon Kligler and the Woodstock Jewish Congregation community have provided a safe, healing and learning space for our family.

People often ask me if I'm proud of my two incredible daughters. Proud is not the word I would use. Looking at the passionate, engaged, caring human beings they've become, my overwhelming feeling is gratitude and a sense of wonder. I hope to never lose sight of the miracle of both of their arrivals.

Marriage and parenting continue to be adventures like no other. I'm a lucky man to have married such an irresistible force. My life partner Julia Indichova has taught me about commitment, courage, sacrifice and unfailingly supported me in becoming my best self. She and I have been blessed with a life for which I never cease to give thanks.

ABOUT THE AUTHOR

Edward Baum is the co-founder of Fertile Heart, L.L.C. a patient driven online community focused on whole-person approaches to reproductive healthcare. He is a graduate of the Culinary Institute of America. His contributions as a chef, musician, videographer, photographer, graphic artist, editor and computer programmer, have made FertileHeart.com one of the most trusted resources for people seeking a health-affirming path to family building. Cooking to Conceive the Inconceivable is a companion book to Inconceivable, written by his wife, fertility educator and advocate Julia Indichova. He lives with his family in New York's Hudson Valley.